Releasing the Scream

Releasing the Scream

Coming to Terms with Childhood Sexual Abuse

Rebecca Newman

HODDER AND STOUGHTON
LONDON SYDNEY AUCKLAND

British Library Cataloguing in Publication Data

ISBN 0 340 58817 9

Typeset by Hewer Text Composition Services, Edinburgh
Printed and bound in Great Britain by
Cox & Wyman, Reading, Berks

Hodder and Stoughton Ltd,
A division of Hodder Headline PLC
338 Euston Road
London NW1 3BH

To Peter
God sent me a rainbow in you,
and a blessing beyond measure.

Preface

This book is an account of my struggle with the effects of sexual abuse in my childhood. It has not been an easy book to write. I have tried to be as honest as I can, and I have asked everyone who has been closely involved with me over the last few years to read it and verify the record. I have gained a lot from writing this account, even though it has been an incredibly painful experience. I could have written the same thing without attempting to publish it, but I have allowed it to become a book because I want to make a difference to other people's lives. I cannot change them of course, but this book is an attempt to point each reader to the God who can.

Also, I cannot offer any solutions, nor can I give you a list of ways of being healed that will work instantly. Most people who have been abused have suffered at the hands of someone to whom they are related, or a close family friend. My experience is unusual in that I was abused by someone who was a stranger initially. I realise that this may make my experience different in some ways to other people's, but I have discovered that the terrible effects of abuse mean that the after-effects have many common strands, regardless of who the abuser was.

By the very nature of the subject-matter, this book is intensely personal. I have, of course, changed some factual details in order to maintain the privacy of those concerned. I have had to write under a pen name, not because I am ashamed in any way of what happened, but because it would be wrong to make my family suffer more by being known. In fact, I would love to be able to write in my own name. I was not to blame for being the victim of abuse, and I have no need to keep it a secret. Indeed, I would like to tell the whole world what has happened and state publicly what has been a secret for too long, but I know that that would be seeking my own healing at others' expense.

The book is not finished. In one sense the sequel has already started, since I am still alive, and I know that God will do more in my life. I am not trying to say I am healed: I am offering the book to you as a gift, a glimpse of the road that I have travelled so far.

1

At last all the children had gone to bed, and I had just enough time to prepare for the next day before Peter and I collapsed into bed ourselves. I had mixed feelings about going out for such a long day. On the one hand, I desperately wanted to go, but on the other, getting up so early in the morning to travel 200 miles seemed to be an awfully big effort to make. It might be a complete waste of time and money, but since it was the first conference of its kind, I had to take the risk. This was something I wanted to be in on right from the beginning.

I laid my suit out on the chair. It showed off my slim shape – despite my having had five children. I was just beginning to feel rather proud of my figure, when I caught sight of myself in the mirror – *that* brought my rapidly inflating ego down to size, and I remembered I was not the spring chicken I used to be! In fact, I ruefully remembered, it was only five months to go until I was forty. The wrinkles were definitely there. I hadn't just got crow's feet, I decided, it rather looked as if the crow had landed from a great height beside my blue eyes. Yes, this was certainly a case for make-up!

I carefully arranged all the various pots of cream and powders that I had accrued over the last few years. I gathered up all the papers for the conference and put them into the smart black leather briefcase that had come through the recycling scheme I ran at the church. I was so pleased with the case. It had never even been used – I can't imagine why anyone wanted to get rid of it – and it instantly made me look like the 'new woman' I so wanted to be on occasions like this. Nothing made me chuckle to myself more than people asking me what my career was when they saw me dressed smartly. I would nonchalantly reply, 'Oh, I am the mother of five children, which is my main career,' and then casually add, 'and in my spare time I teach.' Very rarely could anyone manage not to look flabbergasted about the five children, and I always tried to keep my calmest, most 'got-it-together', face on. Sometimes they would say, 'Oh, I just can't manage with *two* – however do you do it?'

Heavens! If only they could see me now! They would then see that sometimes life isn't always quite so jolly and I am not always quite so calm! One glance in my handbag would definitely indicate a certain lack of something – it often looks like a car boot sale waiting to happen! I can pull out spare knickers in case our youngest one has an 'accident'. There are tissues and tampons by the dozen, because I always put one in 'just in case' – forgetting I do this *every* time I go out! Amid all this, there are endless notes from school – one saying that there's going to be a Book Week, one saying there won't be a sponsored event, one telling me there might be a problem with nits or threadworms! There are also numerous hospital appointment cards for the various ills that my children seem to gather as they get older. I throw out all the irrelevant appointment cards, and then try to tidy the building society books, which I always need with me because I am forever chasing from society to society sorting out accounts to stop us going into the red. No, none of this fits in with 'the image', and I desperately try to sort it all out. Frantically, I ram piles of old tissues and squashed sweets into the waste-paper basket.

I must get to bed, though, as I can feel myself getting to that silly and irrational stage when I feel the urge to start on my now-famous 'Why am I the only one who does anything in this house?' speech – they have all heard it numerous times before. I have to get up at some unearthly hour in the morning for this expedition. I am definitely going to bed.

It was dark and miserable when the alarm sounded rudely. I slowly emerged from under the quilt and looked at the time – I couldn't believe that it was actually five o'clock. I felt as if I had hardly slept at all. I looked across at Peter, who was sleeping peacefully, and wished that I too could just curl up and go back to sleep. The whole house seemed to be so quiet, and with the children so mercifully still, it seemed a shame to have to stir. I glanced across and saw the packed briefcase and the waiting clothes, then slowly stretched a toe from under the duvet.

I felt slightly guilty that I was walking out on them all on a busy Saturday, but I reasoned to myself that it wasn't often that I left the children. If I was honest, they always seemed to have a marvellous time when I went away, and instead of coming home to a husband who was bemoaning his fate, I found that Peter always managed to accomplish far more in the day than I did. I always offered to leave healthy food that was prepared in advance, but, without fail, Peter politely declined. I knew why – lunch was always the same when I wasn't there: one major fry-up with an amnesty operating for any unhealthy food to pop itself into the greasy pan. As for any food with fibre in – well, that was not allowed anywhere near the kitchen, and kept well at bay by copious amounts of tomato ketchup. I smiled to myself. I knew they would all have a brilliant day without me, and I was secretly glad that I was actually dispensable.

I was quite excited at the thought of having time on my own, time out to think about something more stimulating than the whiteness of the wash. I was glad to consider what was happening in the world at large, and I was looking forward to the discussions and conversations that always happen at conferences. The suit looked fine, I put on the make-up, and, even though I knew there were wrinkles, I looked at myself in the mirror and was satisfied with what I saw – well, as satisfied as I am with anything at that time in the morning!

I went downstairs to find that Peter had got up and made me some toast. I gobbled it down – it would have rather wrecked the image to have eaten it as I rushed along the road. Peter, undaunted by the fact that I had toast half hanging out of my mouth in between gulps of tea, prayed with me for the day ahead. We kissed and hugged each other and, narrowly avoiding the trainers in the hallway, the rucksack half spewed out across the porch, and the marks of mud where the children had definitely not heard the order to 'Take those boots off before coming into the house', I ran out to catch the train.

However, I nearly lost my 'got-it-together mother-of-five' image when I realised my watch was nearly five minutes slow – in fact, I had to run like crazy in order to catch the train at all. I got there at the same time that it did and, panting like the very unfit woman that I was, sank in a heap in a corner seat. It took a while before I felt composed enough to get out the agenda for the day. What was the title? 'The First Christian Conference on Sexual Abuse'.

I definitely had mixed feelings about going. I wanted so much to meet others who had been abused to see how they had coped, but on the other hand I was frightened of hearing about their pain. Part of me wanted to share with others my own experience of abuse and the effects it had on my life, but the other part ·didn't want to come out from behind the 'got-it-together' image. Sometimes it hurt just too much. I wanted to hear about what the Church was doing to help people who had been abused, how it was coping with the realisation that so many youngsters are still being abused, and I wanted to find out whether it had even begun to face the ghastly thought that some people in the Church had been, or still were abusers themselves. I have lost count of how many conferences and Christian meetings I have been to, but never have I heard abuse talked about openly. I was so excited at the prospect of a whole day devoted to the subject. I wanted to be part of what the Church was doing, and what it will be doing in the future. Believe me, nothing less major would have dragged me from my bed at such an unearthly hour!

The journey seemed endless, and I wished I had the ability to put my head back and just fall asleep like every other traveller seemed able to do, but I couldn't. My beautifully tidy handbag sat open beside me, and I saw that even that gave clues as to how far I had travelled in coming to terms with the abuse I experienced in my childhood. It had been a long and difficult journey, and at times I wished that I could have just given up, but I knew God was there somewhere and I had to keep going. When I looked at the make-up bag I remembered that ten years ago I would not wear any cosmetics at all – I could not bear to draw attention to my face. At the worst times, I did not want to wear attractive clothes in case people looked at my body. I used to leave my hair long and dangling, not in the neat bob it was now, so that I could flop my head forwards and use my hair as a screen to avoid anyone seeing my eyes. I loathed being on my own in the past, and I would certainly have gone to great lengths to avoid going out for such a long day by myself.

At long last, the train drew in to the station and I gathered my bags together. When I thought about dealing with the effects of abuse in my life, I knew that I would never 'arrive' at my destination in the same final way as the train, but I was now confident that I was a long way on my journey towards healing.

2

I was not sexually abused until I was nearly nine, but the seeds were sown for damage at a much younger age. As I recall the abuse I experienced, it has become increasingly important to me to remember what I was like before that time. Abuse does not happen in isolation – it happens to a child who has his or her own personality, who belongs to a unique family. Even if the abuse that a child experiences is the same, the child is *not* – and therefore the response to it will be different. The type of child may affect the kind of abuse experienced, and the kind of family the child is in will affect the way the abuse is dealt with. The character and experiences of the child before the abuse will also play a very important part in determining how that child copes with the abuse, both at the time it happens and in later life. The only thing that *is* certain in all this, is that no child should *ever* be abused physically, emotionally, or sexually.

I can recall a great deal of my childhood. There were many very happy times, and some intensely sad and frightening times, and all of my childhood affected the woman that I am now. There is no one 'type' of child who is abused; and there is no one sort of family in which it will happen. There are no early experiences that mean that abuse is inevitable. From my own experience, all I can say is that the type of child I was influenced the abuse I experienced, and certainly affected the way I coped with what happened. Abuse happens to a whole person, and the damage of abuse extends to the memories before it happened as well as to everything that occurs subsequently.

I was born one sunny spring afternoon in the early fifties.

My father worked in a small business and my mother was a full-time housewife. I already had a brother, Jonathan, who was three. I have since learned that he was very unimpressed with my arrival, and spent many happy years of my early childhood proving to people in general, and me in particular, just how unhappy he was! Incidentally, it may relieve any harassed parent reading this to know that this part of the story at least has a happy ending – my brother and I now get on brilliantly! Anyway, I was apparently everything that he was not. My mother had found him a difficult and demanding child from the moment he 'landed', whereas I was a very passive, quiet, and 'easy' baby (if there can be such a creation!). I was bouncy and cuddly and learned from an early age that I actually got more attention than my brother by being the opposite of him. (He was loud, noisy, and confident.) However, the consequence of this was that I became more and more shy, and he became more and more noisy.

I was brought up in a busy town for all of my youth, and we lived in a large Edwardian house fairly close to the town centre. We did not have a particularly big garden, but that was where I spent a large portion of my childhood. My parents were both very committed Christians and we all went to the local church. When I was very young we did not have a car. Because we had to walk to church, we went to one nearby. It was rather a dull place – but at least it was close and had a reasonable Sunday school. I was shy, it was true, but generally I was considered to be a 'good' child. In fact, I cannot ever remember being actively disobedient in my early years.

When I was three years old, my mother seemed to 'disappear' for two weeks, and my grandparents, who lived a long way away from us at the seaside, came to look after Jonathan and me. I can't remember much about my mother bringing Lizzie (my new sister!) home, but as far as family tradition has it, I liked her – and Jonathan didn't seem to hate her as much as he had hated me – so we all settled down well together. Lizzie's character was somewhere between

Jonathan and me, so I guess we found some kind of equilibrium when we were all together.

Apart from never wanting to leave the folds of my mother's skirt, I do not have many memories of my first three years. One of the worst ones is of an incident when I was about three and a half. My mother, who subsequently recalled that I seemed to be terrified of needles and injections from the day I was born, had to take me to the doctor's for a routine vaccination.

I sat on the hard wooden stool screaming for all I was worth. I didn't even *want* to stop yelling. If I did, I knew the worst thing – the injection – would happen. I was utterly terrified. Although I was normally so well behaved, when it came to an injection I went wild from fear. My mother tried to explain to me why injections were important; why they were for my own good. I really wanted to be brave, but as soon as I smelt the room, or saw the needle, I was finished.

On this occasion, which stands out clearly in my memory, the doctor announced that I was in such a state that he was not going to do the injection until I had calmed down. So there I was on the stool, yelling and dreading the inevitable. My mother walked across to the other side of the room and she and the doctor talked in quiet tones, waiting for me to regain control. It was a hopeless situation. Although now I realise the room was only a small one, to a three-year-old it seemed huge, and I felt that my mother had left me because I was being so naughty. I was terrified about what the doctor had said, because part of me *wanted* to calm down, but how on earth could I if that meant he would give me the injection anyway?

I felt completely trapped. I knew that nothing I could say or do would stop the inevitable happening. I hated myself, my mother, and the doctor with one huge ball of terrifying hate and fear, but I did not have the words to express any of this. All I could hate was the smell, the loneliness, and the fear that seemed to overwhelm me. From what I can recall, I don't think that I did calm down, but I guess the doctor had a waiting room full of patients and decided he would go ahead anyway. I don't remember that the injection was all that awful – it was the bit beforehand that was so dreadful.

As soon as it was over I calmed down, but it had been a terrible experience, and one I never wanted to repeat. My mother was always kind in that she promised each of us a present if we had 'tried to be good'. I don't remember what she bought me on this occasion, but it must have been hard for her to part with the cash given the disaster I had been! However, she kept her word.

Life carried on as normal, and this major catastrophe in my life did not seem to have any effect on anyone else. When I was young, most of the local children played in the streets, but we were never allowed to. I cannot remember ever wanting to go out – I just loved being at home, playing with my younger sister.

There weren't any playgroups then, so there was never a reason for my mother to leave me – and I don't think she ever let me go to be looked after by anyone else. I used to create such a fuss in the hairdressers' that they always let me have my hair cut sitting on her lap. I had large blue eyes, and as soon as anyone saw the tears form when I was frightened, I was always allowed to stay with Mum! Even in the Sunday school she came with me, and I sat on her lap for the afternoon lessons. We all had books of stickers, but I could only have a sticker if I left her lap and collected it from the front. This was a dilemma indeed. Usually I resolved it by running just as fast as I could, grabbing the sticker, and diving back to the safety of my mother's lap, but sometimes I went without the sticker. I remember that when she stopped to talk to people I hid in the folds of her mid-calf-length skirt, hanging on to her so that she would not leave me. How I envied Jonathan and his confidence, but how opposite I was!

My mother might have taken steps to make me more confident, but we changed to a larger and more active church, and my parents became very involved in it. From the very start, there was a constant trickle of visitors coming to our house. My lack of confidence was never apparent at home – I adored visitors and got on well with them. I enjoyed listening to the grown-ups talking and loved helping round the house when my mother was preparing for them to come.

When I was five, the inevitable happened. No matter how much I wanted to stay at home and play with my toys, the government had decreed that I must be educated. From the very first day I started school, though, I hated it.

My mother would struggle at the school gate with her usually obedient child hanging on for grim death rather than face the awful reality of the huge playground. What a monstrous place it was. There were so many children, so much noise, and I was terrified of being hurt. However, it didn't take me long to discover that the safest place in the playground was walking round with the teacher, holding her hand, and I cannot remember doing anything else in the infant school! In fact, even in the classroom I can only clearly recall sitting on the teacher's lap. I suppose it was because I was such an affectionate and clingy child – so quiet and still when being held, but so unhappy when left alone – that this seemed the easiest way of dealing with me. The only exception to my behaviour was when I was allowed in the 'Play House', and then I was happy because I could pretend I was somewhere else. It was lucky that I happened to be a bright child, because I cannot imagine I learned much at this time!

School was a noisy, impersonal, and smelly place, nothing like the comfort of home. In the infants, when you moved up to the next class, all the teachers went into the large hall and your old teacher walked in with you, then your new teacher walked out with you and took you to your class. Inevitably, my first transfer was from the lap of the first teacher to the lap of the second!

Nowadays, I would probably have been referred to a child psychologist or counsellor, because I was just so unhappy. I wet my knickers on numerous occasions, to the fury of some teachers and my total embarrassment. My mother continued to be very patient with me. However, on one occasion I was so upset, because I had had yet another 'accident', that *no one* at school could pacify me. In desperation, the headmistress let me phone my mother and talk to her! I remember my mother calmly saying on the other end of the phone that she was not cross, and that it was fine to wear my PE knickers, but please would I stop crying and get on with some work. I don't think she realised the depth of the agony I went through at school, because when I was with *her* I was happy.

Sadly, I cannot remember much about my father at this time. The problem was that he had to work very long hours to survive financially. He went to work before the rest of us had breakfast, and didn't return until we were either in bed or just on our way to bed. Since both my parents were involved in the church, they were often at meetings, and Sunday was never a day for seeing a lot of them. They were either very busy or totally exhausted.

The main happy memory I have of being with my father in those early years was when all of us went to stay with my grandparents at their seaside home. One glorious fortnight in every single year Daddy was there and playing with us on the beach. I know my memory is distorted, because on those holidays I can only see the sunshine and the clear water – it never seemed to rain. I remember walking through the dusty, hot streets with metal spades covered in wet sand rubbing against our bare legs, and the metal buckets grating as the handle rubbed against the bucket with the sand trapped between the join. I love to recall walking along with my little hands in his big soft ones, and the special treat of being raised on his shoulders when I was too tired to walk any further, and playing with his tousled hair with my sandy hands. My mother was more relaxed than usual when we were out, and we laughed and played together. My parents would sit on two deckchairs while we played on the beach, making sandcastles and burying each other, or making forts to stop the sea coming in. They took it in turns to watch us, idly chatting with each other while one sat with eyes closed.

These times were like oases in the year, because when we weren't on holiday both my parents worked very hard. There were some very happy times, though. One funny occasion was when we were travelling to our grandparents on the train. It took us all day to get there. First we went on a train into the city, and then we went across London on the Underground, then on to Paddington station where we got on what we called the 'big train'. How I loved that huge, smelly, steamy station and the hustle and bustle. I hated the journey to get that far, but oh, the utter relief to sit down, with the little case I had carried put high on the luggage rack, and to look forward to endless hours of playing games on the train, watching the varying scenery rush past.

On this particular trip, I had wet my knickers while still on the first train. I felt itchy at the top of my legs, but I didn't want to tell my parents. I thought that they just might be annoyed, even though they were generally very patient in that respect. We approached London and the train started to slow down. My father reached up to get down all the cases, I stood up, and my parents noticed the big wet patch on the train seat. Now my father was a perfectionist, and when he was cross he spoke in a particularly precise way. My mother was flapping about getting the cases down and finding knickers amid all the clothes, and my father just said in clipped tones, 'If you *had* to wet your knickers, why did you have to wait until we were near Paddington station? Could you not have done it earlier, or could you not just have waited?' It seems funny that it had not occurred to him to be cross because I had wet my knickers in the first place, but because of the imprecise way in which I had timed it!

Back at home, things were fairly routine. To be fair, with three children under six and church involvement, the word 'routine' can hardly be an apt one, but life jogged along. The highlights for me, apart from the seaside trips, were the school holidays. Lizzie and I were inseparable. Although we both had our own friends, we loved each other's company and never played with other children if it meant leaving the other one out. Our favourite game was 'playing houses'. In the winter we played either under the kitchen table with clothes hanging round, or in our bedroom cupboard, and in the summer we converted the swing into a house. We played every possible game in our houses: our teddies and dolls were patients, pupils, children, Sunday school children, and we swapped between being parents and teachers. I always preferred to be the teacher – despite being shy, I was quietly determined and very bossy. My sister preferred to play nurses and doctors; interestingly, both of us have played our chosen childhood roles in real life as adults.

My older brother seemed to be locked away within himself. He adored reading, and generally was very bright. His games bored us, and he seemed to find us silly. Sometimes he played with us, but he didn't seem to want to play as we did. He was much more into 'Swallows and Amazons' and 'running away from home' games, so we always ended up crying and scared when we had played too long with him!

When I was seven I became severely ill. My mother tried to nurse me at home, but I got progressively worse. I had septicaemia from an internal boil and this had got into my bloodstream. After two weeks, when I vaguely remember being very hot and lying with the curtains half closed most of the time because the light hurt so much, I was admitted to hospital. It hurt if anyone moved me, or even touched the bed. I was too ill to play or do anything at all. When I arrived in hospital after a bumpy and awful journey, I was placed in a large cream-coloured metal cot. Undoubtedly, this was the worst part of the illness. I felt stranded and alone. My mother was sent away and I had to just lie there, hardly knowing what was happening to me.

Not long after my mother left, the sister arrived with a metal bowl and announced that I needed an injection. I was too ill to fight to the extent that I had as a three-year-old, but the abject terror that I felt was no different. However, unlike the doctor in the earlier incident, this sister was angry and abrupt. I was told off for being such a naughty girl, and she then left. My mother was only allowed to see me for three hours every day. It must have been hard for her to stay with me that long when she had the other two to look after, but she was always there. At first she just sat and read to me while I was awake, and then let me sleep, but as I improved we played together.

The timing of all the injections was unbelievably insensitive. Every morning we were given a two-course breakfast, and the first injection came between the two courses. Then after lunch it was compulsory that everyone slept for an hour. The big blue curtains were pulled across the large windows, which was a bit pointless since we were below road level and could only see a huge brick wall and the bottom of car wheels going past. Then we were commanded to sleep. The trouble was that the second drugs round happened halfway through this sleep time, and I was always too scared to go to sleep. I lay in my cot, dreading the sound of the clattering metal medicine trolley. Then followed three glorious hours of visiting, when I would be content once more, and then my mother would disappear yet again through the large double doors. As soon as the parents had gone, though, round they would come again with the medicine trolley and I would have the third injection of the day. From an adult viewpoint, I'm sure those injections saved my life, but all I can remember was a dark and terrible world of fear. I never left my cot to play with the other children, although I talked to some through the bars. I was humiliated by being in a cot at all. Although my mother was allowed to let the bar halfway down, she couldn't cuddle me or hold me properly. When she was gone, I couldn't even reach out for a drink. Once my mother was sitting next to me and was making idle conversation with the nurse nearby. 'Why did they call this ward "Harrington"?' she asked. 'That was the name of the first girl who died in here,' came the reply.

I felt so lonely and everything was so strange, but I didn't realise that I was very close to dying. The problem was that I had not responded to any of the drugs that the doctors had available to them, and if I failed to respond for much longer there would be little hope for me. The church prayed for me (although unfortunately none of them visited me, or supported my parents in more practical ways), and slowly I rallied round.

I then had to have two operations on my face, since there was a fair amount of internal damage, and eventually I was allowed home. I had only been in hospital for three weeks, but it seemed much longer than that. It seemed strange when I saw Jonathan and Lizzie again for the first time. I didn't seem to belong with them any more. It was also odd being home with Dad around at night. He had only been able to visit once, because the visiting times were inflexible and he had to work. I was still very weak and badly damaged by the experience of hospital, and it took a long time to get back to normal.

It was just before my eighth birthday that I was discharged from the hospital completely, and it was about a year after that that I met the person who was to wreak such havoc in my life.

3

Soon after all this, Lizzie and I formed a wonderful club – it was the closest we could get to the clubs described in the adventure books we avidly read. The only problem was that there were only two of us in this club, which did have its limitations! However, I resolved the matter very simply: I was the leader and she was 'the members'. This gave me a justifiable outlet for all my bossiness! There were times when she would not take orders, but on the whole we got on so well together that it was not a problem.

We had rules that we both tried to obey, such as 'Be Kind' and 'Be Helpful', and then we made up codes so that we could write to each other without anyone understanding. We even taught ourselves the alphabet used in British Sign Language, which we discovered in the *Pears Cyclopaedia* we had been given.

This gave us the ability to communicate with each other when we were both supposed to be in bed. My mother seemed to think that when we went to bed we went to sleep, but in fact that was when the 'Butterfly Club' was at its most active! My mother always left the door half ajar, and we would send messages across the room to each other. Sometimes we would play 'gym clubs'. One of us would do a sequence of movements on the bed, then the other one would copy. We certainly learned to be more graceful, because we knew that if we crashed on to the bed, the sound would be heard and we would likely be spanked!

We made pretend money in the club, and pretended our room was a flat. We gave money to each other for jobs we did, and it never seemed to occur to us that the paper money wasn't worth anything. If we ran out, we just made more!

Most of the time the club was good, and my parents did not discourage us. Club activities extended to helping with the cleaning in the house and running to the shops for errands, and so made us more compliant.

What my parents did not realise, though, was that club also meant we did some things they would certainly not have approved of. Sometimes when we were walking to and from school we would do what we called 'tasks' – which was just another word for 'dares'. This meant that we might ring on the doorbell of a house and then run away as fast as we could. Sometimes we went into phone boxes and made annoying calls. We usually ended up giggling, but the seriousness of what we did never entered our heads.

Once we even bought joke cigarettes. They had powder in the end, so that when you blew them it looked as if real smoke was coming out. They were wonderfully realistic. My parents would have had a fit if they had realised that their two darling daughters were walking round apparently smoking. On one occasion a lady stopped us and said that it was disgusting that we were smoking at such a young age. We protested at such an unfair accusation and tried to prove to her that they weren't real cigarettes, but she did not believe us and walked away muttering in fury. We thought it was wonderful, and definitely one of the more successful 'tasks'.

On one particularly sunny day we were going back to school after our midday meal. We always went home for lunch: the school wasn't that far away and Mum seemed to think that unless you had eaten home-cooked meat, two vegetables, and a proper pudding, you were seriously undernourished. We had to walk through a park to get to school, and there were two routes across it. One way was open, and that was the way we were supposed to go. The other way led alongside the backs of garages and a couple of workshops, and we were not allowed to go that way. Needless to say, on this day we decided to do a 'task' and go the 'wrong way'. Anyway, it had always seemed stupid that my mother had said we weren't to go that way. It was, in fact, a slightly quicker route to school, and to us it honestly didn't seem to be that different. However, the fact that it was a forbidden route gave it a certain 'edge', and we decided to try it.

Actually, we were both very disappointed with this expedition. Nothing very different happened at all, and it was rather dull. By the edge of one of the workshops an old man was leaning against the wall, as if basking in the sun. He was dishevelled and looked very old. He didn't have a lot of hair, and the little he did have was white. His face was very crinkled, and he had puffy red eyes. He looked as if he had been crying, for his eyes were very moist. His clothes fitted him appallingly, and his trousers hung loosely at his waist. As we approached him, he turned his creased face towards us, and as we passed by he said, 'Hello'.

'Hello,' we both giggled nervously.

'Are you girls going back to school?'

'Yes,' we giggled again.

'I haven't seen you before, have I?' he continued. 'Well, if you come this way again tomorrow I'll be here, so say "hello" again, won't you? I don't see many people this way and I get very lonely.'

'OK, bye,' we said and ran off to school, skipping together in the afternoon sunshine.

It might not have been exactly what the Famous Five would have classed as an 'adventure', but we were glad we had gone that way. We had managed to make an old man a little bit happy, just as my parents helped other old people.

We resolved that the next day we would go the same way again. It certainly did not seem wrong that we had talked to Mr Sutherland – the saying 'Never talk to strangers' was not so known then. In fact, everything in my experience had meant that we often *did* talk to strangers. People spoke to children in the streets quite often at that time, and it was not unusual to be given sweets. Adults were generally a lot less wary about approaching children. We had clearly been told we were always to walk near main roads, but we didn't know why (it always seemed yet another silly, adult rule), and we also knew that we were never to get in a stranger's car.

After the first act of disobedience, it quickly became the

right and proper thing to go the 'wrong way' round the park, since we felt that caring for this lonely soul must override our parents' rule. Every day we enjoyed chatting to him, and he so obviously enjoyed us going to see him. He told us that we were the highlight of his day, and that made us feel very special. He then asked us if we would go home that way as well, so we could see him twice, and on one occasion when we were going home he invited us in to see his 'woodshed'. We had no idea how big the space was behind the huge garage doors until we went inside. It was just like an Aladdin's cave. Our first impression was the overwhelming smell of wood shavings; we then noticed that they were all over the floor, with lots of sawdust that seemed to form a soft carpet. On one side there was a huge circular saw, and on the other side there were lots of tree pieces leaning against the wall. Apparently his job was to cut large pieces of wood down into thin sticks, and these he bundled up and sold for firewood for 2d. a bundle.

It seemed such a sad and lonely life, and made us realise why he was so glad to see us. He told us that no one came to his shed and that he worked long hours to make enough money to live. In one corner of the shed there was a tiny little room cordoned off with a door. In there it was very warm, because he had a burner that he kept constantly alight with his wood. On this burner he made himself hot drinks using an old metal kettle. There was a dilapidated green armchair in this little section and nothing else. It was filthy throughout – I had never encountered such poverty before, and could not believe that this was his way of life. At first we thought he lived in this place, but then he told us that he had a sister who lived nearby and that he slept there.

On this first occasion as we looked round, he offered us each a sweet, and we suddenly felt as if we'd made a really wonderful discovery. Here we had found a completely new world, and a very special person. After this, we visited him every day, for we realised just how sad he was. We loved visiting him, and it was great to be given sweets as well. One day, he asked us if we had any friends, and said that if we wanted to we could take our friends there as well on our way home.

I was thrilled by this offer. Because I was shy and hated school, I did not have that many friends, but now I felt I had something special to offer them, and we went to school telling our classmates about our new and very secret adventure. For the first time, they were all envious of us, and they too came along.

The five friends we took were all from our Sunday school as well, but they were pledged to secrecy. None of us wanted to tell the grown-ups, because we knew that they were sure to spoil it all somehow. It seemed wonderfully uncomplicated, fun, but grown-ups had a certain way of messing things up. Besides, one of the most fun parts of the whole experience was that we were playing grown-ups and being 'Christian' – we certainly didn't want parents ruining our game. Here at last was a real adult who *needed* us children – it was almost too good to be true. We took our friends into the woodshed, and they were as fascinated as we were by Mr Sutherland's job. He seemed to adore us, and he allowed us to play in the wood shavings as much as we liked. He never chided us, however much mess or noise we made. How unlike home or church that was!

Our new-found friend hugged us, chased us, rolled us, and played hide and seek as well – it was all great fun. Then he told us of another game: he would hold our hands and we would 'climb up' him with our feet and then twirl over. In our innocence we thought this was a wonderful game; we had no idea he was interested in the little bottoms under the pretty summer knickers that he looked at as we turned. To us, it was just a fantastic game. It was like being with Daddy in the summer and I felt the same happiness and relaxation that I experienced then. It was so good to play again after my illness, to be popular at last with the girls from school, and to find someone who thought I was so special.

From an early stage, Mr Sutherland had singled me out. He called me 'Little Becky with the big blue eyes', a title I loved. I had never thought much of myself, and considered I

was rather plain, but he delighted in my face and body and I
seemed to give him pleasure just by being me. I think this was
the first time I had really felt this, and it was a good feeling.
We used to have lots of cuddles and hugs, and Lizzie and I
went back far more often than the other girls. *We* had found
him first, and we were going to look after him the best.

I felt so sad about his lot in life, and wanted to make it all
right for him. I longed to 'sort him out' – I was desperate for
him to come to Jesus and to change his sad face. I wanted
him to know that Jesus loved him, just as I had heard and as
other grown-ups knew. I couldn't believe how much he didn't
know about Jesus and I spent lots of time telling him. Lizzie
and I also wanted to clean up his shed – we wanted to make
everything tidy and clean, like our house and the other houses
we had been in. When we visited him we swept and dusted,
cleaned and sorted. The days went into weeks, and soon a
couple of months had passed. We could hardly remember
our lives before Mr Sutherland; he had become such a good
friend to us.

Then one day he had me on his lap, just the same as
before, but this time I felt his large hand slip under my
skirt and down my knickers. I couldn't quite believe it was
happening. I did not like the feeling of what he was doing,
but I didn't know what to do or say about it. It seemed such
a strange thing for anyone to do. He didn't speak when he
did it, and seemed to carry on as if nothing was happening,
so I pretended too – even though his fat, prodding fingers on
my small and delicate body made me feel very uncomfortable.
He then cuddled Lizzie and I think he did the same to her, but
since only one of us was allowed in the little room at a time
I wasn't sure.

On this particular day, he gave us each some money as we
left. Strangely enough, the money caused more of a problem
at the time than what he had done to me. Obviously, for some
unknown reason, him doing that had given him pleasure, so
that must be all right. But the money! Neither of us knew
what to do with it. There wasn't much money at home, and
we knew that if we got caught with it we would be found

out and wouldn't be able to see Mr Sutherland again. That seemed terrible, so we went to the shops, bought some new plastic mugs, and took them back to our friend. This salved our consciences about the money, and meant that we were able to continue helping him.

From those early stages of abuse, things began to escalate, but only very gradually, and each stage seemed easy to rationalise because it was only a little more than the one before. Yet I dreaded the session behind the closed door. I loathed the indignity of having to have some of my clothes taken off and my body stared at and touched. I was frightened at times of what he might do next, or what would be expected of me. It was the same kind of feeling I had experienced at the doctor's; it had never seemed appropriate to say 'no' to the doctor, and this seemed the same. I felt I had to let Mr Sutherland do whatever he thought was best for me, and, even though I hated it, it did seem to give him enormous pleasure, which I was glad about.

One day when I was in the woodshed he showed me his erect penis. I could not believe the ugliness of this hairy object, for I had never seen anything so ghastly. It looked strangely fresh and young, and didn't look as if it should belong to his old body. It was so big as well. I had heard about boys having penises, but this was quite unbelievable – I was suddenly so relieved to be a girl. He just stood there waving it about and asking me what I thought about it. I wanted to tell him just what I did think and how singularly unimpressed I was, but I knew from his face that he was proud of it, so I said it was lovely and that I liked it. In public, I had heard my parents say they liked things that later we discovered they thought were horrible, but had been too polite to say so. For me, his penis came into the same category, and it never once occurred to me that he was wrong to show it to me.

His hands in my knickers as a quick movement gradually got more extensive too, and he would make me remove my knickers and then rub me and masturbate me until he seemed to be satisfied he had done it enough. It seemed important to him that this gave me pleasure. I hated his dry fingers rubbing relentlessly on my soft, moist skin. It made me so sore, but I didn't know how to make him stop. Usually I closed my eyes and let him get on with it, but on one occasion I could bear it no longer and begged him to stop. However, he carried on – he told me that all normal little girls enjoyed that kind of thing and that I should too. He would only stop when I would say he was making me happy, so that is what I did. He then asked me to touch him, and make him happy. And so on it all went.

It was now more complicated by the fact that he always gave us money, and we had to become even more resourceful as to how to spend it. We bought him food because we thought he was undernourished; we bought him spoons and knives for his shed; we bought sweets and presents for our friends. He made us feel he was being very generous in giving us money. He reminded us just how poor he was, and that he was making great sacrifices to be so generous. We felt bad, but he always insisted that we took the money.

Why didn't we refuse any of this activity? I have asked myself this question over and over again as an adult, and the only answer I have ever come up with is that sexual abuse was not the whole story of the relationship we had with Mr Sutherland. Of all the things he did and was to us, that was the part we hated, but everything else – and that seemed to be the larger part – was wonderful. It was like a price we had to pay for his friendship. In him I found acceptance and understanding. He also gave us time, and played games with us that we enjoyed. He talked to us a lot, and seemed really interested in what was going on in our lives. He wanted us there, we were never in the way, and he was never too busy for us. He was in many ways like a father to us, and I loved being so special to him. The idea of saying 'no' to him for any of his demands simply did not come into it. My parents never seemed to say 'no' to anyone, however unreasonable the demands seemed to us as children, and therefore neither should we. We had always been taught that good children were children who obeyed. I had always had to sit still while doctors and nurses had rammed large needles into my body that hurt dreadfully. How I felt about that experience did not matter; injections were always for 'my good', and Mr Sutherland seemed to think that all he did was for 'my good' as well. Also, I was making him happy, and that seemed to be the thing that children were meant to do for adults. Nothing in the world of the woodshed seemed to be wrong, it fitted in with all that I had been taught and all that I had experienced. Mr Sutherland told us never to tell our parents, because he said that all his life no one had loved him, and that people thought he was a horrible man. Now at last he had found us, and we thought he was special. He didn't want to lose us.

Once Lizzie and I actually decided that we had had enough of him. We had at this stage extended the times we visited him to include Saturdays as well. On that day we were supposed to go to the library and choose our books. What we did instead was to run to the woodshed, spend time with him, then run to the library, grab the first books that we could find, and then run back to give him gifts we had bought him with the money he had given us from the first visit.

Well, we got fed up with all this chasing around and decided we were not going to go that way again. We missed him terribly for three days, and we felt so horrible that we were being mean to him. On the fourth day we could hold out no longer and went back to him. We felt even worse when he cried and cried, and said that he was so desperately worried because we had left him. He told us that he had been so unhappy without us, and we promised him that we would never do it again.

On another occasion some months later, we found to our horror that the woodshed was locked up. After two days, we became very frightened that Mr Sutherland had died or was seriously ill. We considered him a really old man – in fact, he was only sixty-four, but that seemed very old to us. Once he had mentioned where his sister lived, so that night after school we went to his house. When he came to the door and saw us he was horrified, and told us to get out. We saw ourselves as pioneering, caring Christian visitors to the sick, but I now

realise he was terrified we might let out to his sister what
he had been up to.

When he returned to the woodshed he apologised for
being so cross, but said that by going to his house we
had nearly spoiled our special friendship. He told us that
his sister was very mean and horrible and that she would
never understand the fun we had, and that we would all end
up in trouble. As children, we were oblivious to the warning
signs in this statement. In fact, we both concluded that he
needed more visits, because with an awful sister like that he
needed more loving.

However, we could hardly visit him any more often than we
already did. We saw him twice a day on schooldays and once
on Saturdays, and rarely did we manage to avoid him abusing
us in some way. Abuse had become part of our daily routine.
We had known Mr Sutherland for nearly two years, but I knew
that I would have to see him less often. I was going to a new
school, and the route was not the same. Lizzie was still able
to see him, but without me there she went less often.

One day Lizzie rushed in from school, and made it quite
clear that she needed to talk with me alone in our bedroom.
We went upstairs and she shut the door behind her.

'Becky!' she exploded, 'we're going to have to stop seeing
Mr Sutherland for a while. A terrible thing happened to me
today – when I came out of the woodshed, a policeman
stopped me and asked me what I had been doing in there.
It was dreadful! I think we're in dead trouble.'

4

It was as if everything seemed to explode from the woodshed at this point in our lives. From being a secret, it was now something the police were involved with. We were absolutely terrified – we had no one to go to and ask about what might happen. We were very frightened of what our parents might say or do, and this seemed to be in a completely different category from anything we had experienced in our lives before. On the other hand, there was almost a sense of relief that at last things were no longer a secret. The secret had become intolerably big by then. We had grown more and more devious in order to visit Mr Sutherland, and as we got older we felt ourselves increasingly in a situation of blackmail.

It seems strange now, but at the time what Mr Sutherland had done to us was not the important issue for us. What seemed to matter the most was that we had gone the wrong way round the park and had taken money from someone. I told Lizzie that probably nothing would come of the police questions and everything would die down – that after a while we could go back and see him again, but that we just had to keep quiet for a while.

My hope was short-lived. Not long after this, there was a knock on the door and we opened it to find a young policewoman standing there. Mum took her into the living room, and then I was called in to explain what had happened at Mr Sutherland's. It felt like a relief to tell the whole story. I could say it so my Mum could hear it all, and would then understand it. I started to explain about the park, and the first meeting, and the way things had grown completely out of control, but the policewoman interrupted me. She was not

interested in all the complicated details – she just needed
to have some simple facts. Apparently Mr Sutherland was
pleading guilty to whatever it was he was supposed to have
done wrong, and I was not needed as a witness. I just had
to say what he had done to me.

Now this was very difficult, because I did not understand
the meaning of the charge he was on. The policewoman had
said that Mr Sutherland was on charges of 'sexual assault',
but I didn't know what the words meant. I thought it was all
about lying and money, but all she was bothered about was
the touching parts. I couldn't believe it: she simply wasn't
interested in anything else. The actual statement took about
ten minutes: it consisted of where he touched me, how he
touched me, and how he expected me to touch him. The
length of time that this activity had been going on didn't seem
to come into it either. By the end of the chat, she had written
down less than two-thirds of a page. She asked me to sign it,
and then my mother signed it. It was all over.

The policewoman seemed satisfied that I had done all
that was necessary; she didn't pass any comment. No
one displayed any emotion at all. My mother said simply
that I must go and get ready for bed, which I did. Then
the two women stayed together talking. I could hear their
conversational tones as I lay still, but I couldn't make out
what they were saying. I lay in bed trying to make sense
of all that had just happened, but I was unable to. I heard
the door close as the policewoman left. My mother came and
kissed me goodnight, but she said nothing. Her eyes were
red, and she had obviously been crying. I felt horrible.

Lizzie was not interviewed on this occasion – I don't know
why – but a few days later Mum had to take her to the police
station to make her statement. She was terrified and found
the whole experience appalling. She said that they kept using
long words to describe what Mr Sutherland had done to us,
and she didn't understand a lot of what was being said. We
talked together about all we had been asked, and tried to
pin the story together so we could work out exactly what
was happening. We knew that it was something very serious

because the police were involved, and we knew we should never have gone into the woodshed in the first place. We worked out that Mr Sutherland was in some kind of trouble, and we knew for sure that we too were in big trouble for what we had done.

My mother simply told us that my father was never going to know about what had happened. She never spelt out to us what exactly would happen if he did know, but the implication was that it was ghastly. She seemed to imply that she was protecting us by not telling him, and said that there was no need for him to know for it would only upset him. This decision in itself showed us that what had happened was monumentally serious. I had never known anything that she had not told my father – in fact, it was quite the opposite, for they often boasted how happily married they were and how there was nothing they kept from each other.

I cannot now imagine how she kept this from him. How did she manage to hide the pain she experienced, in a relationship that was, as far as I can remember, very open? I can only conclude that, since my father was so busy with his job and with church work, he wasn't aware enough of what she was going through, and that he wasn't close enough to his children emotionally to spot that something awful had happened to them.

My brother was in his element. He kept on and on asking what had happened, and why the police had come. My mother silenced him: 'It doesn't matter what the girls have done. But you are older, and if you ever do anything this awful, you will leave this house.' He didn't find out until our late twenties exactly what had happened.

We were indescribably bewildered. It was like being in a vacuum. We had no one to talk to, and no one came to us. I felt terribly responsible for Lizzie, and felt that it was me who had got her into the mess in the first place. I should have stopped it happening to her, as I was the older sister and was supposed to look after her on the way to school.

Gradually things quietened down, and nothing about it all was mentioned again. We were left with our questions unanswered, and never dared to go through the park to see if Mr Sutherland was still there or not. It seemed that whatever had happened was now all over, and that nothing awful was going to happen to us after all.

Months passed and life carried on as normal. It was a Friday morning, and I was spread-eagled on the floor colouring something. My mother was quietly reading the paper and there was a distant bubbling of lunch cooking in the kitchen. Lizzie was sitting at the table, swinging her legs under the stool while she played with one of her games. Suddenly my mother flung the paper down on to the floor. She was obviously very angry and I jumped with fright. Whatever had I done now?

She jabbed her finger at a five-line article in the paper, and with her teeth tightly gritted she said, '*Now* look what you have done!' My heart started to pound as I read the sentences before me. It read something like this: 'Harrington Magistrates Court sentenced Henry Sutherland (64) to six months' imprisonment, when he was found guilty of nine charges of sexual assault. The girls were all aged between nine and eleven. The judge said, "You have made prostitutes of these girls".'

No sooner had Lizzie and I read these words than she grabbed the paper up again and shouted, 'Don't you *ever* tell anyone about this. I'll hide the paper from your father.' Neither of us spoke. I didn't know what to say. I knew that the word 'prostitute' was somehow the key to the problem, but I wasn't entirely sure what the word meant. However, I knew it meant someone very bad and I realised that if I was the prostitute then I was to blame for what had happened. This was terrible – *I* had done the wrong, and my dear friend who I had loved so passionately was being sent to prison because of me. I wanted to ask my mother what 'sexual assault' meant, but she was in the kitchen carrying on as normal. I desperately wanted someone to tell me exactly what was going on. Why didn't the sweets and the money matter? What had we done that was wrong? I thought that apart from those two issues, we had done the right thing. What I read in the paper was removed from the reality as I saw it. I could not believe what I was reading. Again, nothing was said.

One Sunday evening soon after, I sat at the table drawing a plan of our bedroom. I was always drawing up schemes – this time I was trying to see if I could design a curtain rail that would run across the middle of the room so that my sister and I could have our own rooms. I knew that Mum was not going to be impressed with the idea, but this time I felt I had really come up with an original plan. I eagerly coloured it in and showed her. I had expected an unenthusiastic response, as I was always trying to reorganise things. However, I was completely unprepared for the venomous answer she hissed at me: 'I am not interested in your planning. If you were so clever, and used your brains at all, you would not be in the mess you are now. I don't want your plans. I don't want them!' She rushed out of the room, and I sat staring at the pathetic page I had planned. I couldn't understand what was happening in my world.

I quickly cleared my pencils away and put myself to bed. I lay there, with my face buried in the pillow, sobbing, and trying to hide the noise. What was happening to Mum? She had always been a brilliant mother; she had always been there. She had nursed me through the illness; she had always been listening, tender, and caring. Now suddenly she was like someone else, someone I had never seen before, and I felt it was my fault entirely. I should never have gone to Mr Sutherland in the first place. I should not have allowed him to do what he did to me, because obviously it was a wrong thing that I had allowed. I felt so shabby and wicked inside, and knew that nothing could ever be the same between Mum and me. She knew it was all my fault and she hated me for it.

All this time, it never occurred to me for one moment that Mr Sutherland had done anything wrong at all. I was so frightened for him – I wanted to go and talk to him; I thought he might be able to explain. He had been my closest friend for such a long time – I was sure he would understand something about the situation that my parents and the police obviously did not. I was scared that people would hurt him – he was so old – and I knew that I would never see him again. I felt as if he had died and yet I knew he was out there alive somewhere. I did not even know exactly where. There was no one to talk to. I dared not speak to God about what was happening – it was obviously too awful for him to understand or help. I didn't know what to think, how to feel, or what to do.

I pause momentarily between sobs and listen intently for the sound of my mother's footsteps on the stairs. I am sure she will come and listen. She must.

She always has. But there is nothing, only the resounding sound of silence, interrupted by the uncontrollable sobs coming from inside me.

A great fear is within my body, a new kind of fear. I have never experienced fear to this depth before. Bewilderment fills every part of my thin frame. I must never speak to anyone about what has happened. I know that this awful feeling will be with me for ever, and there will never be an answer to the questions that I am asking. If I cry for long enough I am sure the tears will eventually stop. If Mum sees my pain, she surely must reach out to me in the end. There must be someone who will listen? Surely someone out there will try to understand? But what is it that I want anyone to understand? If I don't know myself, how can anyone else?

I want to scream, 'Please, someone take the pain away from me! However wicked I have been, I can't live with this inside me. Won't you please just punish me in any way that you want to?' Any punishment would be better than no communication at all, and would at least have an ending. The awful truth slowly dawns on me. I have done something so awful that my punishment will be eternal silence.

I can only scream a noiseless scream, only cry without tears, hurt inside, but make no display of pain. I hunch myself on the bed, hold my legs tight to my chest, curling up in a small ball. I try to hug the pain and comfort myself. In the loneliness of the long night, I fall asleep.

*   *   *

Inevitably the sleep could not last for ever and the morning came. I got up and carried on as normal. Everyone else acted as if nothing had happened, but part of me was left on the bed. No one would ever reach that part of me. No one would hold me. No one would love the child I had left behind. From the outside I looked the same, a pretty child with large, staring blue eyes and short, blonde bobbed hair. My shy awkwardness had not changed. I was a sensitive and easily damaged child still, and that was no different. But from that moment onwards, I knew that nothing in my behaviour must show what had happened inside me.

What I had done felt so terrible that I did not dare give anyone the slightest clue. If they found out what had happened, then the consequences would be so far-reaching that they could be worse than what I had already done. I had to leave Becky frozen. I had to leave her behind. I could not embrace her, or listen to her in any way. I could no longer handle how she felt or what she had experienced. Quickly I learned the skills that meant I was able to hide behind the flimsy mask of normality.

The Becky who had been abused was, as far as I was concerned, now dead.

5

The first major event that happened after this time was in my spiritual life, when my mother took me to see a film about Christianity. This was about a year after the abuse had been discovered, when I was twelve. Mum had resumed her normal caring and loving relationship with me, but had drawn an invisible veil around the experience of abuse. I realised that as long as I never mentioned it, everything would be all right. I knew that my father had been told nothing about it, so it became increasingly easy to carry on, and almost believe that nothing serious had ever happened. My mother seemed to have forgotten about it, so I just had to do the same.

I got on well with both my parents on these unspoken conditions. My father had changed his job and this meant we saw much more of him. At this stage he began to take far more interest in our lives, and this became the basis for our relationship as adults. He saw more of my mother and, although they were both still heavily involved in the church, we children were quite happy, since we now had a new minister, Sam, who involved us in all that was going on. We had youth activities and meetings, and generally I was at the stage where I was glad to be more independent of my family.

On the day I saw the film I was stopped dead in my tracks. I had always considered myself to be a 'good Christian'; it seemed that as far as possible I had kept all the rules and been a very conforming child. The point of the film, however, was that people had to make a personal commitment to the Lord Jesus Christ. Going to church, doing the right things, and trying to keep the rules was not enough: it was to do with a personal relationship. I could not believe that the film was correct. I was very distressed at the thought that if it was correct, I was not actually a Christian. I asked my mother when we got home if I was a Christian, and she said simply, 'No, you are not. Just because your dad and I are, doesn't make you one, but if you have decided for yourself that you want to ask Jesus into your life, you can.'

I did not hesitate – of course it was what I wanted. I immediately realised I had been missing out. It then dawned on me, as my mother prayed with me, that Jesus dying on the cross was for me too. I could have eternal life. Suddenly, the meaningless phrases that I had recited endlessly in Sunday school seemed to make sense. I *knew* I was now a Christian.

Nothing stunning happened. I thought that from that time onwards I would be good, that I would no longer want to sin, that my life would be straightforward. I had no inkling that that would not be the case. I do not even remember thinking about the abuse at all, then. Although it was only a year after the discovery, I had successfully erased it from my memory.

Being a Christian did not change the loathing I felt about school. I went to a very mediocre 'all girls' school, with rules that were outdated and an education that matched the old-fashioned uniform. I hated the other girls – all they talked about was sex and boys and their latest conquests. They laughed at me, thinking I was different because I was a Christian. Also, I was very thin and not as physically developed as they were. My breasts did not seem eager to appear and my periods did not start until I was in the sixth form. My classmates ridiculed my underdeveloped state mercilessly, and since we had to queue for showers it was quite obvious that little was happening! On one occasion I confided in my older brother about how awful they were to me. He suggested that the next time we lined up for showers, I was to make sure that I was the first in. Then I was to walk through the showers backwards, tilting the numerous spray heads upwards to the ceiling as I went. This meant that my hair stayed dry and everyone else was soaked. My brother could be so understanding and practical at times like these!

The next week I decided to try it, and it was even more successful than I had hoped. The other girls made such a fuss about their hair getting soaked that they all got told off. The teacher didn't notice that I was the only one who didn't look like a drowned rat, and for one brief second I felt I had the victory!

It was only short-lived, though, and nothing I could do would make me popular. I was not as streetwise as they were; I was not given the freedom in the evenings that they had; I did not understand half the things they talked about or the words that they used. In fact, I did not fit in at all. This would not have been so bad if I had excelled in the academic side of things. However, I did not feel particularly intelligent, and felt I must have got into grammar school by mistake. I had to struggle with all that I learned. I worked very hard on my homework, and learned that study was a useful solace in times of pain. For two years I struggled on being quiet and shy, and all the while hating it. It was then that I discovered a side to my personality that was a lot more popular and fun to be with: the rebel.

I knew that I had good qualities of leadership, and I also discovered that the headmistress had banned the school Christian Union when it had became too 'evangelical'. This appealed to me immensely, so I set up a secret Christian Union at my house, which was close to the school. We put up secret notices on the blackboards with codes known only by people who were involved. There could be no public announcements, of course, and this added to the secrecy and fun of it all. Even if the headmistress found out, there was little she could do, since the meetings were held at my house. My parents were very supportive, and I enjoyed leading the meetings and getting so many new people in. More girls became Christians and others began to put the faith of their upbringing into practice. I organised visiting speakers and loved the activity of it all. I was sometimes allowed to read passages of Scripture or parts of books in assembly. Once I stood up and read a piece that I had written myself, and the headmistress was so angry that she refused to let me speak again in public unless she had previously read what I was going to say.

My leadership qualities, though, also had a bad side. I wanted to challenge a lot of what I was learning, and much of the way that teachers handled the classes. I had always hated school, and now in my mid-teens I discovered I could argue back. Sometimes I would just organise girls into refusing to do things, or diverting the teacher away from the task in hand. We played tricks on the teachers, I chatted in lessons, chewed sweets, and looked and spoke insolently. I was a really horrible person to teach, but I was leading a kind of double life, since I was also professing to be a Christian. In church I was quite different, and they could not have imagined how I swore as much as the other girls at school yet was well spoken at home.

I don't know how much of the roller-coaster experience I had as a teenager was a direct result of the abuse I had experienced, or how much of it was a response to the anger and fear inside me. I have since taught teenagers myself and am bringing up some of my own, and much of what I experienced seems typical of many young people.

It was for me a very lonely time, though. I didn't like much of what I was, but I didn't seem to have the power to become the person I wanted to. I could not control the anger inside me, either about myself or about others. I could not understand the way that I behaved at times. There seemed to be such extremes to my personality that at times I could hardly believe they were all in the same body. I was struggling to discover the woman inside me, to find out who I was for myself, rather than the image others wanted me to have.

In my late teens I tried to talk to Sam about how awful I was and how horrible I felt inside, but he could not relate to it. He just kept telling me how great I was in the church, how much good work I had done in the Christian Union, how God was using me then, and would continue to use me in the future. The more I begged him to listen to the darker side of my personality, the more he said I was just being humble and I was failing to see myself as I really was. I wanted to believe what he said was true, but I lived with the other half of me and knew that it was not.

I'll never know quite how I managed to leave the school with nine 'O' levels and three 'A' levels, all with good grades. I fully expected to fail everything I ever took, and the exam results were the first indication I had that I was not as stupid as I believed. The school was shocked too – and no one had even thought about discussing with me the possibility of going to university. I don't think anyone expected that I would get good enough grades. I had always wanted to be a teacher, and had been accepted by a teacher training college. There was a lot of talk in the school about the girls who did go to university, particularly Cambridge and Oxford, but the rest of us were thought of as those girls who didn't quite make it.

I was certainly a very mixed-up teenager, but I put it all down to being at an awful school. I fervently hoped that when I went to college, things would be very different.

6

However, college came as a shock to me, for I had not reckoned on being nearly as homesick as I was. I missed my family dreadfully, and the new church that I went to was nothing like the one I had come from. I didn't feel I fitted in at all.

I changed my name when I went to college, for I found out that the name 'Becky' had been used in the past to describe a local prostitute of some renown. The information really alarmed me, but I didn't know why. All I knew was that from that minute on I hated my name, and so as soon as I left home I deliberately became 'Rebecca', and would not allow anyone to use the shortened form again. I now realise I was trying to separate myself from my past and become someone else, but at the time I wasn't conscious of this.

I adored the work at college, and generally I was better behaved. I really wanted to be a teacher, and knew I had to pass everything on the course. I studied Theology and Education as my two main subjects. Rather than rebelling as much in outward ways, I resorted to argument and debate – this seemed to be a much more socially acceptable approach. But how I argued! It didn't matter who said what: I had to disagree. I hated authority or leadership in any shape or form. I felt that someone else was trying to control me, and I couldn't bear it.

On the face of things, I was at the centre of most action. I was heavily involved with the Christian Union, and my room at college was constantly full of people, generally those with problems. I was at my happiest surrounded by people. I worked very hard as well, in between serving cups of coffee, and even did extra work if I didn't feel stretched enough. I began to replicate my parents' house, and my father's way of throwing himself into work. I totally ignored how I felt. Sometimes I felt very depressed and often very lonely, but busyness became my solution.

The highlights at college were the teaching practices, where I discovered that I could relate to children very well and just loved being with them. I could make school into a fun experience, and the children could still learn. My deep yearning to be a teacher was going to be fulfilled and I was doing well in my studies. On one occasion, as part of our course, we had to produce a tape of poems and music. I greatly enjoyed preparing mine, and went to the lesson keen to share it with the others. English was fun and I enjoyed the group I was with. When it came to my turn however, I simply could not let the tape be played. I dreaded anyone hearing what was on it, and could not understand why. The tutor could see I was genuinely upset about it, and offered either to let me have the tape back or listen to it herself at home. She did the latter and then talked to me about it.

The theme of the presentation was loneliness. When the tutor heard the tape she realised that what had started as an academic exercise had ended up as a cry from the heart. I could not let my friends hear how I felt – they would never understand that underneath the extrovert exterior was a very lonely person. I had the reputation of being the student you went to if you needed help, and I myself perpetuated this image. In reality, I was probably one of the students in the greatest need of help. I had not learned to relate to anyone in any other way then helping. This wasn't actually wrong in itself, but the danger was that I was trying to help them from a life that was so badly damaged that I did not have the resources to cope with their problems. In fact, their problems dulled my own pain: I felt so sad for some of them that I did not have to think about my own disquieted feelings. Even though I was such a public Christian, I could not pray for myself. I also made sure I was hardly ever alone, for on the occasions when I was, I found myself very withdrawn and depressed. When the door was shut at night, I felt very unhappy.

One way in which I found relief from my inner tension was to do outlandish things or play practical jokes. I organised sponsored events in aid of charity, such as holding all the tutors hostage for a lunchtime. In a less generous frame of mind, I once organised a group of friends to put clingfilm across every toilet one lunchtime, and then we all stood back and awaited the hilarious consequences – needless to say, there was complete uproar before the afternoon lectures. I was never found out for that prank, or the many others that I played!

While I was at college I had many opportunities to chat with lecturers, and baby-sat on several occasions for one of them. She knew that I was very unhappy, but no one ever seemed to be able to understand what was wrong, least of all myself. I spent endless hours talking to the co-ordinator of the College Christian Unions in our area, and always seemed to be in a state of doubt and despair about my faith. He attributed it all to the fact that I was studying Theology and, worse still, Philosophy. He said I thought about everything too much, and just needed to get back to a simple faith. This was what I desperately wanted to do. What I did not realise then was that the 'simple faith' I had held as a child had got me into dire circumstances, and the only way I could have a faith at all was to be as complicated about it as possible. I needed, I felt, to find a faith that would not be so badly hurt again. I had a terrible picture of God from the start, but I did not realise it, and this was not to emerge for many years.

The co-ordinator and others prayed with me. One couple 'cast out the demon of doubt' and others just told me to believe. I was tossed around inwardly, and still didn't know who I was; I felt I was scum and valueless. However, there was one young man from our home church who did not share my opinion of myself, and that was Peter.

I had several boyfriends during my teenage years; some lasted a short time and others for quite a while. I always thought they were 'Mr Right' for a while, but after a time I got fed up with them and finished the relationship. In the church I was brought up in it wasn't difficult, as there were so many young people – we just swapped around when we got fed up! None of us took the relationship side of things very seriously.

I went out with Peter for nine months, and in that short time I knew he was different from all the others. Although he was the exact opposite of me, I respected him in a way I had never respected any other man before. He was gentle and quiet, and I was by now noisy and extrovert. I led from the front, and thought that was what leadership was about. He led quietly, but in a very strong way. I made a lot of fuss about what would happen next. He simply made sure that what he wanted happened anyway, no matter what noise I made! He was a very considerate person, always caring for my welfare. He listened to me – really listened – and was wonderful to talk to. In fact, we spent much of our courtship just talking. I think he was the first man since Mr Sutherland that I spent such a lot of time with, and who I was gradually able to trust. However, I never told Peter of the abuse – by this time, I seemed to have erased all memories of it. It just didn't seem to be a part of my life.

Peter and I got engaged in our final year. While we completed our degrees, we lived quite a distance apart, but we wrote daily and phoned each other every other day. The relationship was very special, and we both felt that God had set us apart for each other. I had always thought that I would marry an extreme extrovert who would be a church leader of some kind, but Peter was the opposite to all that I had imagined. I am so glad that God led me to such an open and gentle man. I would probably never have learned to trust any other man in the way I was able to trust Peter. He was so dependable – the constant factor that held my roller-coaster life together. I doubt if my marriage would have survived if I had married the kind of man I initially thought was best for me.

It was not long, though, before it was clear that the memories of the abuse had not been entirely obliterated. For ten years I had coped with all that had happened by wiping it away, and for the following fifteen years I went into complete denial of all that had passed. Every event that might have served to point towards the damage done to me by Mr Sutherland, I bypassed and explained in other terms. Perhaps an appropriate title for this book would have been 'If only I knew then what I know now'. All that had happened to me was still there, though. I could not bury Becky or leave her frozen for ever, and what she had experienced had to be dealt with.

7

We were both very excited at the prospect of getting married, and everything seemed to be perfect. We loved each other very much, we had somewhere to live, we had completed our training, and both had careers to start. What more could we want? How easy it was to vow 'for better or for worse', yet, as I look back over seventeen years of married life, I marvel at how little we understood the implications of those words. We went to the minister for a chat before the wedding and he said that if we wanted to talk to him about anything that worried us he was available. We didn't think, then, there was anything we needed to know. How wrong we were!

I had spent all my teenage years asserting that when I got married I would be a virgin. I had read the Bible on the subject and concluded that sex was a special gift from God, designed for the context of marriage. It seemed common sense to wait. This decision made things a lot easier for me when there was pressure from boyfriends to go a little too far. I knew that I certainly wasn't prepared to, and however much I wanted to have more fun at the time, I was utterly determined to wait. This made me the butt of many jokes at school. The other girls laughed so much when they wanted to know about my sexual experience and found out that, as far as I was concerned, there hadn't been any. Every girl had her own tale about 'losing her virginity', each one seeking to be more sensational, than her peers. I felt so isolated, and at the time naïvely believed their stories. It was tempting at times to make up a tale just to keep them quiet!

I don't know exactly what I expected sex to be like. I knew it was meant to be special, something very enjoyable for both of us. I knew the basic mechanics of the act of intercourse, and various bits of complicated gossip picked up from school, but apart from that I didn't know a lot. I presumed my husband would know more – unfortunately, he didn't. Neither set of parents had talked about it at all with us, apart from very basic details when we had been much younger. We hadn't been given any books on the subject either. My mother had always said she would answer any questions I had, but I didn't know what I was supposed to ask.

We arrived at the hotel for our honeymoon. The wedding had been wonderful, everything we had dreamed of, and great fun. However, we both felt quite lonely in the expensive hotel where we spent the first night, and quite out of depth in such a place. Everything felt so strange.

On our wedding night, we undressed and got ready for bed. I put on the pretty nightdress I had saved for the occasion, and then we started to caress each other for the first time in the parts of our bodies that had previously been out of bounds. Everything felt beautiful and right. Our ignorance may even have been to our advantage, because we had the chance to discover each other with a freshness that education might have spoiled.

Suddenly, though, I froze inside, and wanted to push Peter away with all my might. I felt terrified of him, yet strangely I wanted him to be violent rather than gentle. I desperately wanted him to hold me, but simultaneously I didn't want him near me at all. Everything was the opposite to what either of us would have expected and I couldn't believe what was happening. I dissolved into floods of tears. Peter reached out and held me, and comforted me until we both fell asleep.

I woke up in dread of the rest of the honeymoon. What on earth was wrong with me? I had spent so many years saying 'no' to sex that I didn't have a clue how to say 'yes'. It had not dawned on me, as it has now, that the night of the honeymoon was the first time that a man had tried to touch me in the same place that Mr Sutherland had touched me. Although my mind had tried to blot out the experience, Peter had brought it all back. Subconsciously, it seems I had made the decision that I would never allow anyone to touch me again like that: I could not say 'no' before, but now I was able to, I was certainly going to exercise that right.

In a less than jubilant mood, we both went down to breakfast. My face was puffy from crying and neither of us had slept well. It was not the start we had prayed for, or expected. After breakfast, Peter announced that he was going to pray about the situation. This, he stated, was the first problem in our married life, and since we wanted God to be involved in everything we had to pray about it. I was so embarrassed – I had never prayed about anything like that before, and it seemed awful even to mention the subject to God. It might have been possible to imagine praying about it by myself, but *together*? That was almost unthinkable. However, Peter was adamant, in his usual quiet way, and proceeded to pray. He asked God to help us in this area. Inwardly I was trying to imagine how on earth God could answer such a prayer – the possibilities seemed quite irreverent! However, Peter was confident that God would sort it out. Neither of us realised then that this prayer was going to be prayed many times during our married life.

The next time we cuddled, Peter went more slowly and we finally managed full intercourse. I was so relieved that we had, as I regarded it then, been 'successful', for I had feared coming home from the honeymoon feeling a complete failure. The strange thing we discovered was that I enjoyed the actual act of intercourse very much – it was the foreplay that completely terrified me. I could not bring myself to touch Peter, and I could hardly bear to look at him either. I honestly thought that I was mentally unbalanced, because I had never heard of anyone with sexual problems and thought I must be the only woman in the world who was not normal. Having been at school with girls who made out that sex was the simplest thing on earth, I was completely unprepared for a problem. In the end, Peter and I muddled along in an unconventional fashion for the honeymoon and actually had a great time, apart from the disastrous start.

When the honeymoon came to an end, we returned home to set up our first flat. It was all much more difficult than I had imagined it would be. Our new careers took up so much time, and I had never before had to organise such a lot in a house, since I had been in a small single room at college. We were also attending a new church, which didn't seem to be anything like our old one, and both of us were pretty homesick.

The job I had for my first year of teaching was a good one. I was Head of Department in Religious Studies with one man working under me. This might have been acceptable, were it not for my appalling attitude to authority. I was excellent at leading, and had new ideas and plenty of enthusiasm. I proved myself quite successfully to the pupils, but I was hopeless at being led by those above me. In college my attitude had not caused any problems, as questioning and arguing were encouraged. Out in the real world of work, though, it wasn't quite as acceptable. I would not be told anything; I was pig-headed, arrogant, and incredibly strong-willed. Even I was surprised at my own attitude. I felt so angry at those above me: even though they were helpful and supportive, I could not accept their authority.

With hindsight, I realise that their basic failing as far as I was concerned was that they were men! In the school hierarchy there were three men who were senior to me, and I didn't want them controlling me in any way. I almost cringe as I write this seventeen years later, when the links between my abuse and my behaviour are so horribly obvious. However, at that time I did not even have a hint of understanding.

The situation was so bad that the Inspector of Religious Studies came to visit me, and watch me teach. He said he was most impressed – he loved my approach and I was an excellent teacher. Then came the sting. He explained that he had been talking to the head teacher and was concerned about my attitude towards those above me. I did not seem to take any orders, he said, and explained that I would not be a good leader for long if I didn't change. I was desperately embarrassed, because I had not appreciated how badly I was behaving. He said that he felt I wouldn't listen to men, and asked me if there was any man I respected and would listen to. 'Yes,' I retorted aggressively, 'my husband. He is the only one who I will ever listen to.'

That night I got home from school and was flabbergasted to discover that the Inspector had left the school and gone straight to where Peter worked to talk to him. He explained the situation and begged Peter to talk to me, because he said there might be serious problems if I didn't change. I could not believe how serious it was, but obviously it must have been for the Inspector to take such drastic and unprecedented action. It was clear that I had to learn to be much more humble – and very quickly. I don't really think any of my underlying attitudes changed, but I managed to start asking the men for advice and help, and consulting them about what I was doing. The Inspector, it seems, had managed to save me just in time! Peter was bemused that I had said I would not listen to anyone except him, but I felt humiliated by the whole episode.

I not only found settling into a new job difficult, but the new church was very hard for me as well. Everything and everyone was different. In my home church I was well known, since everyone knew my parents, and people just accepted me as I was. Now, though, Peter and I had to make our own identity as a couple. This was made harder by the strong pressure from the church for us to do every job that there was. Within the first six months of arriving we were asked to teach in the Sunday school, run the youth work, get involved with the Brigades, and many more minor activities. Since we didn't have any children and we were both keen to work in the church, it seemed obvious to many that we must be 'called' to each of these roles. It didn't seem to occur to anyone that it was all we could do to get to church some Sundays because we were so tired! We worked every evening until very late just to keep our jobs ticking over.

I was partly to blame for people expecting so much of us, because I presented myself as very confident and coping. I was inwardly struggling with most areas of my life, but I was too scared to show this to anyone. We started to open our house as my parents had done, and often had people round from the church. We did a great deal of entertaining, and left ourselves little time to adjust to each other. Peter had been brought up in a quiet home and he loved to be able to invite lots of people for the first time.

We were too far away from our old church for anyone close to us to see any danger signs, and the sexual side of our relationship was suffering terribly. Because of these difficulties, I just tried to avoid the subject – and the activity itself! Keeping busy, as always, became the way to avoid looking at any inner hurt.

It might seem a strange thing to say, but apart from our serious sexual difficulties we were incredibly happy in every other respect. We enjoyed being together, and found our opposite characters were beginning to complement each other more and more. Neither of us was disappointed in the other, although there were many adjustments to be made.

Our only rows, which were fairly frequent and serious, were about sex, for I had begun to feel completely inadequate and different to everyone else. When I watched television I could find nothing to match my experience, for women always seemed to be happy about sex. No one else seemed to have any practical difficulties in making love instantly, and thinking it was wonderful. By this stage in my marriage, I found the whole experience distasteful and frightening. This all served to confirm my inner suspicion that I was very odd – I was just not the same as anyone else.

Peter was always gentle and never once became aggressive for his own satisfaction. This must have been quite difficult for him at times. He was, after all, a normal, healthy young man, and he could reasonably hope to make love to the woman he loved and had married – who loved him dearly in return and who actually wanted to make love too! Neither of us could understand how we could be so happy with each other outside the sexual relationship, and yet so unhappy within it. Just as my mother had done, I had drawn an invisible circle round sexual activities, and for me it had become a kind of Jekyll and Hyde experience.

We struggled on like this for eighteen months, and then one day I happened to see on the top shelf of a Christian bookshop a book called *Intended for Pleasure*. I took it down and studied it. I could not believe at this stage that the word 'pleasure' would even appear in the same sentence as the word 'sex', so we bought the book and both read it avidly.

This might seem obvious to anyone else, but I was shocked to discover that sex was designed for mutual enjoyment. I had certainly lost sight of that through my experience. I was acting as if Peter was the one who was odd, as if he was over-demanding just for his own satisfaction. He frequently told me that he just wanted me to be happy, but I could not believe that. All those years ago Mr Sutherland had kept saying that all he did was for my happiness. This I knew to be a lie, but I had absorbed it inwardly, and would not trust another man in this area. If I had made that connection then, we would have been a long way towards dealing with some of the issues. However, at the time, I made no connection at all.

After one particularly vehement argument about sex, I told Peter that there wasn't anything really wrong – it was simply the contraceptive methods that we were using. I then concluded that if we used the rhythm method we might see an improvement. Catholics advocate this method as a means of birth control, so we went to the Catholic Marriage Advisory Council for help. All we were interested in finding out was how you could stop conception by taking your temperature every day. Fortunately for us, the doctor not only gave us the charts, the thermometer, and some information, but she also took an active interest in us.

We spent our first visit talking with the doctor about lots of different things and she asked us to fill in the charts for three months and then go back to her. When we did go back, she was horrified at the erratic results. Not only were my monthly cycles of wildly varying lengths, but the temperature revealed nothing at all because it was all over the chart. I think she thought we were not following the instructions properly, because she explained it all again to us in very simple language and told us to try again! Three months later, we went back once more.

Since the doctor we were seeing was also trained in relationship counselling, she looked further than the immediate difficulties we had with the chart and enabled us instead to talk about the problems in our sexual relationship. It felt such a relief to be able to talk to someone else other than each other. As I verbalised our sexual problems, I slowly began to remember the incidents with Mr Sutherland, and started for the first time to catch a glimmer of a connection between our sexual problems and the abuse. Until this time, I had still not even connected that there was anything sexual in what Mr Sutherland had done. No one had explained to me what the words in the newspaper meant. What had happened to me had been when I was a child, and I did not realise that that would affect me as an adult.

As I was thinking all this, the ghastly truth dawned on me that I had never even mentioned it to Peter. I could not begin to face telling him, because I still remembered the injunction from my mother that I should never tell anyone because there would be dire consequences if I did.

At this point, the doctor, as if reading my mind, said she felt there was something I needed to tell Peter. It was by then late in the evening, so she suggested that we went home and returned the following week to talk about it. Peter didn't have a clue what was going on in my head.

The whole of the week I was in a terrible turmoil, and feared it would be the end of my marriage when Peter found out what a dreadful thing I had done. Would he want to stay married to a woman who had been a girl prostitute, I wondered? I feared he would not. I now realise how deeply all the earlier experiences had affected me, for there was nothing in our relationship or Peter's character that suggested he would ever walk out on me like that.

I felt so nervous as we drove to see the doctor at the end of the following week. My hands were sweaty and, although I tried to rehearse how I would tell Peter, I could hardly even imagine the words to use. Thirteen years had gone by since the abuse, and I had never spoken a word. How could I begin now? How could I tell Peter it was all my fault? Would he be able to go on loving me? Was this the end of our relationship? All these questions swirled frantically in my head as we entered the doctor's room.

8

I cannot remember how I finally managed to blurt out what had happened to me. There was so much to explain, such a lot I wanted to say. I simply spoke the facts about the abuse, and then waited for the response I dreaded. The response I feared was not there, though. Instead, Peter just reached out to me, as I was hunched up and crying by the time I had finished, and could not even look up. Gently, he held me and said, 'You poor darling.'

The doctor said quietly, 'That was an awful thing to have happened to you.'

Then I realised with horror they had not understood the situation at all. 'It was *my* fault, don't you understand?' I blurted.

'It was not your fault,' said the doctor gently. 'It was *his* fault.'

I could not believe the words I was hearing. How could she possibly think it was his fault?

'I wish my mother had punished me then, instead of telling me to be quiet!' I retorted.

'Why should your mother have punished you?' she replied. 'You did not do anything wrong.'

Peter kept trying to reassure me that what she said was true. It seemed impossible to accept so simply, even though I would have loved to have believed it.

I was so glad to speak, and the relief I felt at telling what had happened to me was so immense that it is quite indescribable. I had spoken the unspeakable, defied my mother's threats, and discovered that, if anything, my marriage was stronger than ever. The reality was that no one had rejected me and my mother had been wrong. I felt free, whole, and complete.

I suddenly felt in control of my life, and not living under fear of discovery. I felt confident that we would be able to sort out our sexual problems now that we had both seen the immediate connection.

Unfortunately, my enthusiasm and feelings of exultation deluded the doctor into thinking she had been like a fairy godmother who had solved our problems in an instant. Years later, I discovered to my cost that admitting what had happened was only the first step in my healing. I needed a lot more help in coming to terms with the extreme damage that had been caused; there could never be a 'magic wand' in that respect. Peter and I hardly saw this doctor/counsellor again after that. I didn't need the birth control charts anyway. – in my usual headstrong manner, as I thought everything was sorted, we started to plan our first child!

There was one major obstacle on the horizon if we were to have a baby: my terror of needles. Only anyone who has been totally petrified of something can begin to understand how crippling a phobia is. I am not talking about just being scared, but of being so frightened of something that you change the course of your life to avoid that object. As I mentioned earlier, my fear of needles had started as a young child and had been made worse by the experiences of early vaccinations. At the age of seven it had virtually taken root with the time spent in hospital. Needles meant only one thing to me: the power held over me by the person controlling the needle.

I cannot blame Mr Sutherland for causing my fear of needles. However, in practice the phobia became an outlet for expressing my feelings about the abuse. I think that my fear would have stayed within the normal ranges were it not for the fact that I was then abused. Abuse was a major experience that was similar to having an injection: I was helpless, out of control and feeling pain, at the mercy of an adult. Consequently, later in life these two experiences became inseparably linked.

Of course, none of this was at a conscious level at all – it is only now that I can see the patterns. At that time, I saw every difficulty that I had as being separate from other problems – my difficulty with men in authority, my poor view of myself, my fear of needles, my hatred of sex. It is so much clearer today that these were comparatively common problems, but magnified out of all proportion as a direct result of the abuse. The only common factor that I could see then was that I was at the centre of them all, so I concluded that I must be the one who was odd, because nothing seemed to make sense. Other women did not seem to be the same as me – *I* had to try harder to change. As you read the next few chapters, you may wonder what on earth all that follows has got to do with abuse – at the time I couldn't see the connection either, and neither could anyone else who tried to help me.

My main regret is that I did not know then what I know now. If I had, I would have gone for immediate professional counselling, or possibly even psychiatric help, to sort out the damage Mr Sutherland had done. The other issues would then have changed. However, my ignorance of the subject meant that I went about it all the wrong way, and one of the reasons I have written this book is that someone reading it may get the help they need sooner rather than later – and maybe will be spared much heartache and pain.

The only word that can describe the following fifteen years is denial. To survive, I denied the pain and the effects of the abuse. The way I saw it was that the abuse was dealt with because I had named it, and that seemed enough. As far as I was concerned, I now had to sort out the phobia of needles, and that seemed to me a lot more serious!

My teenage years had been made even more miserable by this phobia. Sewing lessons were a perfect nightmare – so many needles were being let loose in the room at one time. I was always scared someone would come towards me with a needle, and I could never concentrate on what I was doing because I spent most of my time looking round to check that I was safe. I resorted to messing about in all the lessons and trying to distract the other girls, since this at least kept their minds off their needles and meant I was safe. I was not popular with the old sewing teacher, who missed most of my dramatic antics because of her poor vision. One day she asked me to put the ironing board down. My mother ironed on a blanket on a table, and I didn't know how to do it; so rather than ask anyone, I undid the bolts on the legs and watched the entire contraption collapse, much to the fury of the teacher and the amusement of my peers!

I also hated sport. I could not bear to get involved in anything too violent, because I knew that if I was injured I would need a tetanus injection. That thought was too terrifying for words. In hockey, for example, I was always given the post of winger, which I was glad about as it kept me out of most danger. I was often shouted at, because on the rare occasions when the ball thundered across the pitch I was so scared of being hurt that I jumped over it. I cowered if girls came towards me with their sticks. The only area in which I performed reasonably well was running, because then I was by myself and moderately in control.

I was so embarrassed at my ineptitude – which I don't think can be entirely blamed on the phobia – that I messed around in lessons even more. There was one occasion when everyone was watching me being taught how to throw the discus. You are meant to swing round three times and then throw it. I felt so stupid being watched that I started to mess around, and in my confusion swung round three and a half times before letting go. The PE teacher was livid and sent me indoors. I had thrown the discus straight at the crowd of watching girls and had only narrowly avoided hitting them.

Anyway, the time had come to face the fact that if I was ever going to produce a baby I would need some kind of injection. I had read as many baby books as I could, and could not find any that avoided blood tests during the pregnancy or injections in labour. Even the most 'natural' childbirth books managed some injections, and I just knew I couldn't become pregnant until this phobia was sorted out. I had to conquer my fear as I was desperate to have a baby – I adored children, and was prepared to go through anything to have my own. Eventually we shared the problem with one couple in the church, and they urged us to get help immediately. I decided then that I needed to find someone whom I could trust and then ask for help. So one evening I went back to my home church to talk to my old minister, Sam. At that time, our own church didn't have its own minister.

Sam was very patient with me as I tried to explain the problem. The difficulty was that I could not bring myself to tell him exactly what I was frightened of. It was so terrifying that I could not even say the word 'needle'. It sounds ridiculous now, but I was afraid that if he knew what I was scared of he would have power over me, and would use his knowledge to control me. Eventually he worked out what the problem was, and said he would think about what help I needed. I was singularly unimpressed – I had hoped he would say that he would pray for me, even lay hands on me, ask God to remove the fear, and then I would be fine. It sounds incredibly simplistic now, but I had no idea how deep the roots of my phobia went, and how much needed to be dealt with to sort it out. Sam, it later turned out, had decided that I needed professional help, and intended to find out what was available before we met again. I, however, was looking for a quick spiritual answer, so felt very disappointed.

After our chat we went to the prayer meeting. My mother was ill at this time, so both parents were preoccupied. I felt so ashamed that I was such a useless person – I didn't know of any other Christians who had such a terrible fear of anything. Even Sam was surprised at me, as he had known me since I was twelve. He had always thought of me as coping and energetic, and on many occasions we had deep and lively discussions about many issues. He was upset that he had been my pastor for so long and only now had I told him of this deep and secret fear.

He said that he had tried to get close to me emotionally, but always found us to be a 'closed family'. We dealt with everything between ourselves, so he thought I would not have kept such a problem unresolved. He had seen our 'open house' and had mistaken it for 'open emotions', but the reverse was true: what we could do for others we could not do for ourselves.

My parents did not exclude us from discussion, but never did they raise the issue of my phobia. I think they hoped I would just grow out of it – I don't think they wanted to admit that one of their children was seemingly so irrational – and I was never encouraged to talk to anyone outside the family. In practice, I was actively *dis*couraged – my mother always reminded me that other people were too busy and had enough problems of their own without hearing about mine. It seems as if my parents felt threatened if we discussed them, or anything about each other, outside of the family. There was such a strong sense of loyalty. I did not understand then that parents often do not see how much their children need help in some areas – I believed I lived in a perfect home, and had never learned that different people have varying ways of handling situations.

Sam had no idea of the torment I had faced in the early years of my marriage. He had never known about the abuse, and I didn't mention it now. It seemed to pale into relative insignificance in comparison with the pressing issue of my needle phobia.

At the prayer meeting there was a prophecy from someone, and I felt God speaking directly into my situation. I knew that the woman praying could not possibly have an idea of what I had just shared with Sam, since I had stayed with him the whole time. The prophecy was this: 'God says, "Your healing will come, but it is not going to come in the way that you want it to. Healing for you will be slow and hard. You must remember that from where I see things it is different and you are going to have to trust me".' The person praying then went on to describe a picture she had of a huge, craggy rock face with someone trying to get along the middle of it without falling into the sea below. This person was attempting to climb to the top to be rescued from the cliff face. From where God was, at the top, the path looked very clear, but from where the, person was, it seemed perilously obscure. God then promised that when the healing came it would be complete.

At that time, I was not very aware of what people describe

as 'spiritual gifts'. All I knew was that someone had said something that was relevant to the situation I found myself in. Anyway, I thought that all I needed to deal with was the phobia, so this prophecy just made me think it might be less than instant. I had no idea how long it was all going to take. I wanted some sort of healing, but God, who had known everything that had happened to me since the day I was conceived, wanted to heal me completely. Only he knew how much there was to deal with, and just how much help I was going to need. I think if I had known the way ahead, I might have been tempted to give up and settle for a life of childless celibacy! However, I had sincerely asked God to heal me and I desperately wanted to change, so I thought I was prepared for whatever it took. I was sadly mistaken.

9

I was headstrong and stubborn to an extreme degree and this served to make the next few years of my life even more difficult than they might have been. I knew that I was due to see Sam ten days after the prayer meeting, but I wanted to get my 'healing' over and done with – I simply could not see the point of waiting a moment longer. I know that I had been terrified for the past twenty-two years, but I naïvely thought I could sort it out myself if I made more effort.

On the first Friday evening after I had talked with Sam, I was at home on my own as Peter was on a course some distance away and wouldn't be back until later. I never really liked being on my own, but I just felt that this time I was going to make myself think about all those things I had refused to think about for so many years. I rang Sam and announced my intention. I was not asking for his advice – I simply said that I wanted to have a focus for my thoughts. He suggested that I wrote about the first memory I had of having an injection. I went into the lounge and sat at the typewriter. This was it, I thought. I will face this fear head on. The problem, of course, was that I had no idea of the vast amount of damage that the fear of needles was masking.

I started to type. I wrote about the feeling of isolation as I waited for the injection, and my mother walking away from me, the terrible fear . . . suddenly I couldn't type another word. I was utterly terrified. The memory of what had happened was not only so powerful, but all the associated feelings of terror flooded over me. I stared in disbelief at the words I had written. I couldn't even read them, yet it was as if they had a power of their own. I just couldn't stay in the house with them. I got up and fled outside. I rushed round to Jean's and Fraser's house. They attended the same church as us, and were the only people who knew about my fear of needles.

My intention when I arrived was to explain to them just what had happened. I felt I could then be rational about it all, and everything would be all right. The events that followed, however, changed how the matter was resolved in a major way. By the time I arrived at the house, I'd calmed down and carried on as if everything was fine. I found I did not want to tell them how frightened I had been, because in the security of their lounge it all seemed so silly.

I sat down; Fraser was changing the nappy of their eighteen-month-old daughter. He had lost the pin, and he and Jean were looking for it. Suddenly the terror flooded back. A pin lost in the room! What if someone found it and attacked me? While Fraser went on searching for the pin, Jean resumed sewing the leather coat she was trying to mend. The needle would not go through and she kept on saying, 'I just can't move this needle. It's stuck'. The words froze inside me.

I tried to concentrate on the television to keep calm, and to my complete horror the story on the news was about an immunisation programme that was being started. Needless to say, they showed people having injections. By now, the fear I felt had grown so much I could not even begin to express it. The television was turned off. Jean put her sewing down. The little one was put to bed, and Fraser turned to me to chat. 'Are you OK?' he said.

I wanted to scream at them for help. I wanted to reach out to them and be comforted. To my amazement, when I tried to open my mouth to speak, no sound came out. I tried to move my body and it was as if I was completely locked up. Then inside a kind of shaking started that spread and spread until I could not move at all except for shaking from head to foot.

Fraser and Jean were horrified. They had no idea what was going on, but seemed to think that *I* did, and that I could control it if I wanted to. I wanted to push Fraser away from me – I saw him as the enemy, and yet needed him as a friend. What on earth was happening to me? I had never heard of anything like this. The fear I was experiencing was so much greater than anything I had known before in any circumstance. It was just raw terror, and there was nothing to cling on to for an explanation. It was a fear so big that it appeared to assume an identity of its own.

Part of me could think coldly and rationally, but I did not seem to be able to connect that with the rest of my mind or body. I could hear everything that was being said, but I could not relate it to my actions. I was desperate for someone to hold me, but if Fraser moved towards me I recoiled so much from him that he had to back away. I could not even bear to open my eyes.

Fraser was, understandably, becoming more frantic. The anxiety in his words and tone of voice made me feel even more frightened, and he told me that I would have to go into a psychiatric hospital if I carried on behaving in this way. Although his words and tone of voice were understandable, they were less than helpful. I was already totally convinced that I was going out of my mind, and this is how I imagined it felt to be on the edge of complete madness.

This bizarre situation went on for about an hour. By this time, Peter had got back, and Fraser rang him to say I needed to be taken home. Unbelievably, when Peter walked in, I went back to being completely fine – or so it seemed. I looked a wreck, admittedly, but I could look at Peter and move. Fraser and Jean felt very bewildered and presumed I had done this before and that Peter would know what to do, and how to get help for me. Nothing, of course, could have been further from the truth. Peter thought that Fraser and I had been arguing, and that I had simply lost my temper.

While we were driving home in the car, Peter asked me what had happened. I told him that I didn't want to talk about it, and we drove me home in silence. When we walked into the lounge, I found the sight of the typewriter very distressing and asked Peter to remove it. Both feeling drained, we went to bed.

This had been my first attempt at examining my own feelings about the past, and it had been a resounding disaster.

I spent a restless night becoming more and more locked into myself. I tried to explain to Peter what had happened, but we were both bewildered. Peter told everyone who called the next day that I had a migraine. I was still so distressed by Monday that I felt unable to go to work, so Peter contacted the doctor and briefly explained the situation. She said that she would have to see me, but agreed to cover over all the instruments in her room, because I was too terrified to go in there otherwise.

When the doctor heard the details, she concluded it was an anxiety, or panic, attack. She prescribed medication to reduce the immediate level of fear, and said I needed psychiatric assessment and help. I was so relieved to hear this, because I feared that when she saw me she would have me admitted immediately to a psychiatric hospital and that I would never come out again.

As far as I was concerned, the medication had a wonderful effect. Unfortunately, though, no one realised at first that I was very sensitive to these tablets and that the ordinary dose was far too high. I was in a twilight haze for four days, hardly moving off the settee. A psychiatrist then came to the house and told me I must come off the medication straight away. He said he would make an appointment for me to see a behaviour therapist, who would help me get rid of the fear of needles as soon as possible.

However, as the drug wore off, a very strange thing seemed to have happened. Needles did not seem to be nearly so terrifying – instead, I became petrified at the prospect of being left alone. I made sure that either I had visitors or I had somewhere to go. If neither of these options was possible, I would wander round the streets rather than stay alone.

I felt so ashamed of this new difficulty – it seemed as if I was making up problem after problem simply to get attention. In reality, I would have been glad of no attention at all if I could have eradicated the inner torment I was experiencing. I did not know who I was any more. I was no longer in control of myself, something I had always prided myself on being.

Having learned so well to give help, I now found out how inadequate I was at receiving help from others. I did not know how to admit how desperate I was, and put enormous energy into covering up how I felt. Yet I still tried to be available for others in need, because that was the only way I could get respite from my own inner pain.

I tried to keep going as normal, and kept attending church, although it was almost a waste of time. My goal was simply to get to church, last through the service, and leave again without anyone getting close to me. If people asked me how I was, I could not physically look at them. If someone reached out to touch me, I moved away.

People began to get impatient with me, because I seemed so inexplicably changed. I was moody, depressed, and tense. I became even more bossy and overbearing than usual, trying desperately to avoid being controlled by anyone. Yet I was so frightened that the church would reject me completely. Much of the time I was at home I was crying, and as much time as I could I spent being busy. I was physically exhausted, but threw myself into my job with more vigour than ever before.

At this time, there was a student at our school who was trying to assess the amount of stress that teachers suffered as a result of their work. For his project, he measured all the pulses of the staff before and after each lesson. Everyone on the staff performed as he had anticipated, but the poor young man was baffled by my results. The more stressful the lesson, the lower my pulse went, and the more relaxed the environment, the higher it went. Of course, the harder the task in hand, the less I was having to push away the fear that was constantly with me, but as soon as I sat quietly drinking coffee, for instance, the fear was much worse.

I contacted Sam and unfairly blamed him for landing me in such a mess. I asked him whether he thought I should go for professional help or not bother. He said that, since this was the way things had turned out, I should go along with it. He offered to counsel me about spiritual things if necessary, but felt the phobia side now had to be dealt with by someone else.

I went to the behaviour therapist, a young man called Brian. He had been trained as a psychiatric nurse primarily, and now had diverted into this kind of work. He was full of enthusiasm and utterly convinced that behaviour therapy was the cure for everything. As the name indicates, behaviour therapy aims to solve people's problems by helping them to change the way in which they behave. The problem for me was that the issues I was presenting with were not the underlying problems at all, but a superficial mask for the deeper damage of abuse. I did not realise that all the pain I was to experience in this therapy was only going to relieve a symptom and not a cause. I would never say that behaviour therapy is wrong for everyone. It can be a brilliant part of healing, but for me it complicated things yet further.

By now I felt as if my life was entirely falling apart, and I clung to behaviour therapy as if it were a lifeline. It seemed to me to be my only hope of making it through. It was clear to Brian that I was not functioning well at home, although school was all right and gave me a useful focus. He tried many different ways of encouraging me to stay by myself. He tried to get me to increase the time spent alone, from one minute to two, and so on. The trouble was that, however much I convinced myself I had to stay alone, I just watched the clock until I could run out. I still hated myself, and despised my own body. I didn't want to live in me. These feelings were so deep that it didn't matter how much I sat alone – it made no difference.

I could not by this time look at myself in a mirror either, for I could not bear to see the pain in my eyes. Brian tried to make me look in a mirror and only succeeded in producing yet another terrible panic attack. Looking back now, the link between my abuse and my behaviour then is just so clear; I can hardly believe that no one spotted it or attempted to help in a less superficial way.

It was desperately unfortunate that my behaviour therapist was a man, since I just saw all he was doing to me as abusive.

He did little to help, since he often hugged me and comforted me at the worse times. I have subsequently found out that this is not typical or appropriate practice, so I would not want to put anyone else off by the fact that I was being dealt with by a less than helpful therapist. He told me how attractive he found me, and said that this was part of improving my self-image. He asked me to dress more attractively for him, and said this was all part of my therapy. He admired any efforts I made with my dangling hair, which I had now grown long in order to hide my face. Brian saw this all in terms of my therapy.

However, to me it felt like a double message: this man only wants to help you for his own satisfaction; you are really just as ugly and dirty as you thought you were before. The problem was that nothing was different inside, whatever I changed on the surface.

One day Brian shut me in a room with a two-way mirror and said that I had to be there all day alone – he did not care if I panicked or not. By this stage he had got fed up with the gentle approach, and decided to try the 'flooding technique'. The principle behind this is that the brain is so flooded with fear that it goes into overload, and afterwards the fear is no longer there. The idea was that having survived a day, I could survive anything less much more easily.

It was an absolutely desperate day. I coped by clinging on to myself as best I could emotionally. I counted the specks on the wall; I prayed.

By this stage, I was already seventeen weeks' pregnant with our first child. I cheated with the 'flooding technique' because I worked out that actually I was *not* alone in the room – I had a baby there with me. I managed to last the day without a panic attack and went home. Brian proclaimed it was a success, but inwardly I felt more locked in and very depressed.

Two weeks later, Brian was moving on in his methods yet again. He decided that the 'gentle approach' to the needles situation was also not working, and booked one complete day when he would give me injections continuously. He said that he would ignore all panic attacks and keep on and on talking about needles. I felt desperate and wanted to refuse, but the first blood test I was supposed to have was in two weeks' time, and I had to have the test done for the baby's sake.

By now, I was emotionally in a terrible mess. I was terrified of needles, I was scared of being alone, I hated myself with an utter loathing, and I was very depressed. Therapy seemed to have made everything more complex, but I now seemed to have no alternative but to go through with Brian's plan – which to me felt like an invitation to hell.

10

The day that Brian flooded me with injections is a day I wish I could forget, but it will be etched in my memory for ever. It was almost unimaginable to me to be faced so violently with the very thing I had fought so hard to avoid.

I knew I was terrified of needles, but did not realise until much later that the feelings concerning my abuse that this fear was masking were being made far worse by the whole desensitising experience. I was stuck in a room for a whole day with a man who kept giving me injections without emotion and without appearing bothered about how I responded. Although I wasn't consciously aware of the connection, it felt like the abuse happening to me all over again. I could not run out, just as I hadn't been able to as a child. I felt as if my views were unimportant: I simply had to sit there and put up with it. The same message was being given – you must accept this because I have decided that it is best for you.

I felt torn inside. I wanted to scream, hit, and push Brian away, but on the other hand I could not continue through life with this terrible fear of injections and needles. Although I had intellectually agreed to this process, I had not at all understood how awful it would be. By the end of the day I felt senseless. I didn't care who I was any more, or that I was pregnant. I wanted to disappear and hated myself even more, because I felt it was my own weakness that had made me have to go through such a situation. When I came home from the hospital, I was so deeply depressed that I wondered if I would ever be the same again. I felt more locked into myself and confused than ever before. The only plus factor was that when I had the blood test at the hospital the following week, it seemed like nothing in comparison with that terror-filled day. However, I had paid a very high price to get rid of my fear. I had dreamed that when that fear had gone I would be 'normal', fearless, able to cope – everything I hadn't been for so long. It is true that I had lost the fear of needles, but I had also hidden part of myself even further away.

At about this time, a group of friends in the church became very concerned about the way I was behaving. They were increasingly aware of the gap between the coping and energetic person that I was some days and the depressive, frightened woman they saw if they got any closer to me. I didn't realise that anyone had noticed anything at all, and thought that my cover-up act was quite successful.

If there was any activity at the church I was always involved in the organisation behind it – I wanted to be in control. I planned sponsored events to raise money, and other activities. Peter and I were the youth leaders in the church, so we spent lots of time with the young people. They often came to our house and we organised trips and activities for them. If anyone was ill, I was there visiting them. I baked endless cakes and meals for anyone in need. I could not stop serving people, both in the church and in the community. If I heard of any problem, large or small, I wanted to help put it right. I drove people to hospitals, to visit relatives, to do their shopping. I did anything that would stop me from sitting at home and being depressed.

Now there was nothing wrong in what I was actually doing, but my motivation was definitely dangerous. I was not *entirely* covering up, for I did love being with people and I genuinely wanted to help them. I really wanted them to see God's love in action. The trouble lay in the fact that I was doing everything out of an empty and badly damaged heart, and was terrified of stopping my busyness. I could not bear to be alone, for fear that I would have to think about myself. Everything I did had 100 per cent of my energy and devotion, and there was no space left for God to reach in and heal me. I was so frightened of any more pain, and could not understand how I had been through so much in behaviour therapy, yet just seemed to be getting worse.

One particular evening I was desperately restless. Even though Peter was in the house I just could not bear to be sitting still. I was too exhausted to bake another thing, and I suggested to Peter that we go out to visit someone in the fellowship. He tried to convince me to stay at home, but I wasn't listening, and insisted on going out. We drove round to the houses of all our closest friends, but no one was in. Finally, I suggested we went to Jean's and Fraser's home. When we got there, I noticed the cars of all our friends parked outside. Why were we being left out? I was hurt and wondered what we had not been invited to.

'Shall we go in?' I asked Peter. He looked very uncomfortable, and I knew he was hiding something from me. I begged him to tell me what it was, and he admitted that he had been told that a group of people in the church had been so concerned about me that they had decided to meet together for the evening to pray. I was furious, for it felt like an infringement on my personal life. How dare anyone sit and discuss how I was behaving! I questioned how they could tell Peter something that he had to keep a secret from me. I did not appreciate then how desperately in need of support Peter was, and how much he needed to know that he wasn't alone. I felt humiliated and foolish. We drove home and I went straight to bed.

Years later, I look back on that time with such gratitude. I now cannot believe how caring those people were that they took the trouble to meet together for my sake. I thank God that they were prepared to pray for help, rather than just muddling on and doing more damage. I never did find out whether the Lord gave them a mighty revelation about my problems on that night. He certainly didn't give me any!

In practical terms, though, I now had no support at all. Brian, the behaviour therapist, had left, pronouncing that I was cured and that he had been successful. There was no follow-up, and no assessment of whether his view was correct. I was now capable of having an injection, so everyone considered that my sole problem had been cured.

*   *   *

The summer holidays were approaching, and I was beginning to feel excited about being pregnant. With the therapy behind me, I looked forward to the baby's arrival just before Christmas. It was also our third wedding anniversary, and Peter took me away for a week's holiday as a surprise present. It was very romantic, and I began to feel that perhaps the depression would lift after all.

Little did I know what severe problems lay ahead. On our return, Peter decided to decorate the house, ready for our new arrival. While in the middle of this job, he ran out of paint, so popped out on his motorbike to get some more. While he was gone, I took myself to bed for an afternoon rest.

I was suddenly awoken with the noise of persistent knocking on the front door: it was the police. Apparently, the motorbike had skidded on some oil and Peter was being rushed into intensive care with severe head injuries. I arrived at the hospital feeling devastated. Whereas before I would have been too scared even to go to the hospital, I was at least grateful that I did not have to give it a second thought.

When I saw Peter my heart sank, for I could see that he was in a critical condition. He was moaning, but not fully conscious. The X-rays showed he had fractured his skull. Provided nothing went wrong, the doctor assured me that he would be home quite soon. In fact, he was on the critical list for three days, and during that time his condition did not improve as expected. I spent as much time as I could with him. I felt so grateful that God seemed so close to me at this time. I did not know if Peter would die; I did not know what our future held, but I was so confident in God's promise to be with me whatever happened, that I found a new and deep calmness that I had never felt before. I could even hold Peter while he had injections.

Friends both within the church and outside it were wonderfully supportive. The family all rallied round, and I experienced so much loving care that I did not anticipate the difficult time that would lie ahead. However, Peter was still not improving – if anything, his condition was deteriorating. On the third day, further tests revealed that a large clot had formed on the brain and he needed immediate surgery. The clot was successfully removed, and I was desperately relieved to be told he would recover. I was not given any other information.

After this, Peter seemed a lot better, and after two more weeks they allowed him home. He was thrilled to be back, but I could not express my inner fears to anyone. He simply wasn't the same person who had left the house to get paint that tragic afternoon.

In recent years I have contacted the organisation Headway, a support group for people who have head injuries, and for their families. Unfortunately, it hadn't been formed at the time of Peter's accident. I have since found out that emotional damage is the last aspect of head injuries to be repaired, and that the people the injured person cares about most are often the ones they find it hardest to relate to.

At the time, I did not have the words or the understanding to express what the problem was with Peter. It just seemed as if he was completely without any emotion when he was with me. He seemed to get on fine with others in superficial ways, but he could not see why I needed to be cuddled or kissed, and did not know how to comfort me if I was upset. He even failed to understand why the baby's arrival was important. It had also taken him a few weeks to remember that I was his wife and that I was carrying his child. He wasn't physically aggressive, but from being a very caring and open kind of man, he had become completely selfish and locked into himself.

I could not bear the new Peter, and sought to do anything I could to bring him back to his old self, whatever that might cost. I discovered that visitors helped him, so I arranged a constant flow of people to come to the house. We shared all our meals with others, and I threw a party and invited forty guests. I tried to piece together the parts of his past that he could not properly remember. I did all I possibly could, but he did not change significantly. He was still without emotion towards me.

I felt desperate. People in the church added to the pressure, although unintentionally. They said things about how wonderful it was that he was healed; how marvellous he was looking; how blessed I was to have him home. Yet I needed to express the inexpressible: I had lost my husband weeks before. The man I was left with spoke the same, looked the same, but to me he was not the same at all. Part of me even wished that he had died, because this experience was like a living death.

Peter himself seemed oblivious – he was happy in his childlike way. I started to have terrible panic attacks, and I got to the stage where I didn't want the baby to be born. I felt as if I could not face anything traumatic. I could not cope with a husband who was so changed and a new baby. Eventually I was taken into the ante-natal ward for a rest.

In the church I felt that only Jean and Fraser had understood the changes in Peter, for they were close enough to see how different he was towards me. They had him to live with them for a while, and the hospital even suggested that he should not have open access visiting.

Then, amazingly, his brain seemed to be triggered on a pathway back to relative normality. While I was in hospital and not there for him, he began to miss me. Very gradually, he wanted to know about the forthcoming baby. Slowly, he wanted to relate to me. One of the most memorable experiences was when, after five days of being apart, a nurse let him listen to the heartbeat of our child. His face lit up for the first time since the accident, and he said gently, 'That's our baby'. I burst into tears of sheer joy that he understood at last. The nurse rushed out and told all the others. Everyone had been so supportive and upset by our situation, and there was excited pandemonium as people started to realise that Peter was going to be all right. I knew then that we would make it, whatever it took. After five more days, we were back at home together, and although he was only gradually improving, every day brought me a little closer to the man I had married.

After what had been a horrendous pregnancy, Samuel arrived with comparative ease after a mercifully short labour the week before Christmas. Peter was pleased, and I was thrilled. He tried to think up surprises for my homecoming, but he was still so unwell that he told me everything he had done each time he visited me, and did not realise that it was no longer a secret – just as a three-year-old might behave. I had to come home and pretend to be surprised at everything, and it wasn't an easy time. On the day Samuel was born, Peter brought me a single red rose. I was so touched, and hoped dearly that this was a sign that he really was getting better. I asked him why he had brought it for me. I desperately hoped he would say that it was because he loved me, and was thrilled about Samuel. His answer was typical of his state at the time: 'Well, the people who brought me here in the car stopped outside the florist on the way. They told me that you have to buy flowers if your wife has a baby. I didn't know why, but I did it because they said so.' My heart sank.

If I had been a 'natural' mother I might have found the months that followed easier. I thought that if I could cope with classes of secondary pupils, one little child would be easy. Nothing, however, had prepared me for motherhood.

11

I could not believe the amount of work and fuss one small body could create. I had read all the books on what to do but, the problem was that Samuel didn't seem to have read the *same* books! I thought I would have lots of spare time between feeds and changing to do things for myself. Instead, I found I could hardly get a meal on the table. Most of the time, the house looked as if a family of pigs lived in it. I wanted to be organised, but the baby was unpredictable and seemed to mess up anything I tried to take control of.

I felt inadequate, and unlike the other women I saw pushing their babies around in prams – they all seemed to be coping. Peter had gone back to work, but since he was still quite different he did not take as much of an interest in Samuel as I needed. I felt I had to tell him everything that needed to be done as he seemed to have lost all initiative. He couldn't even remember two requests in sequence, which proved infuriating. I would say something like, 'Could you go upstairs and bring down the change of clothes and put the wash box back?' He might manage to accomplish one or the other, but rarely both. I ended up having to write endless lists for everything. Peter was convinced I was being silly, but I was so frustrated at his poor memory. He didn't seem to be bothered – and I felt at times as if I had *two* children rather than one. He was also very absorbed in his work, as he had to try very hard to remember all that he had forgotten.

At about this time, a new pastor and his wife arrived at the church. They were expecting their first baby and we started to get to know them. It was their first pastorate, but it didn't take Stephen long to realise that I needed help. He offered to see me to chat about the difficulties I was having. At the time

I started to see him, we wrote down a list of all the areas I found hard.

I was horrified at the nature of the list: I hated myself; I could not bear to be living in my body; I didn't like the way I looked; I despised the way I acted, and the constant feeling of being driven by an inner force – having lost the ability to say 'no' to anyone or anything. I hated my bossiness and my need to be in control of all situations. I was angry that I did not seem able to relate to God, and although I could pray for everyone else's problems, I still could not mention any of my own. I could not be still for any time at all. I felt hunted within myself, as if by an unseen and unnamed enemy. I could not look at anyone directly if I felt they were being too probing, especially men. I did not want men in particular to touch me or move towards me, and I was still having panic attacks when Fraser was around. He sometimes became too probing in his attempt to help me, and that just terrified me, although I gave out the message that I wanted his help. I hated the name 'Becky' and reacted with terror if anyone used that name by mistake. I did not feel I was coping with Peter and the change in his personality, and I was angry at what had happened. I felt useless because of the long periods of depression I experienced, and I was tense and anxious all the time. I could not relax or enjoy my husband or child, or even myself. The list was endless: I felt such a failure.

Stephen felt that he could help me, but he said it would take time. I was to go and see him every fortnight and we would talk through the areas on the list. If Stephen had received better training in the area of sexual abuse, or even if he had encountered it before, he might have been able to deduce from the list that there must have been some experience that was underlying all the symptoms I described to him.

Unfortunately, we both thought that if we dealt with each symptom in turn, I would be free to live normally. Stephen did not probe behind the issues to see if there was a first cause. Later on, when I had read extensively on the subject, I discovered to my relief that instead of being totally irrational, as I had considered myself then, I was displaying very common after-effects of sexual abuse, and that many others have shown similar symptoms.

The next five years were spent largely in counselling, with Stephen trying to keep me going, and nothing deeply changing. The good thing was that he did clear away a lot of the problems, so that when I was ready to deal with the abuse there was less to be dealt with. I have nothing but admiration for Stephen and his wife Lois for their faithfulness and kindness to me over those five years. They really were trying to do the best for me, and I was not an easy person to counsel. I could never blame Stephen for failing to wonder if there was a reason behind all the symptoms. As I presented it to him then, I had just been through intense and painful therapy to remove a lifelong phobia. My husband had just recovered from major brain surgery and was still acting strangely. I had just become a mother. I can see why he thought it was hardly surprising I also had panic attacks and got very depressed!

The counselling was not all intense, for Peter and I had a developing friendship with Stephen and Lois that survives to this day. Counselling was kept separate from the rest of our lives, although at times that was difficult. It was also very hard to be counselled by the pastor, in the respect that I had to see him every Sunday as well as at some mid-week meetings. I did not like the fact that he knew so much about me. I also had the problem that when he was preaching, it felt as if he was getting at me indirectly. I had become extremely sensitive and felt there was no privacy, nowhere I could go to forget the parts of me I hated so much.

I shudder as I remember the panic attacks. Every time Stephen tried to deal with a particular issue I would start to block off emotionally, and never knew why I did it. At one level I knew Stephen was my friend and that he was trying to help me, but at a deeper level I wanted to stop him, to make him go away. I felt a terrible, mindless fear that I could not name. I would close my eyes and find my body locked up. I could not speak, although words would be going round and round my head, and I didn't seem able to stop them. I could not understand how sometimes a situation did not make me panic, and then a seemingly identical one would.

I did not realise then how much, for me, counselling by a man resembled at a subconscious level so much of the original abuse. I panicked if I caught sight of his eyes watching me. I felt terror that I was causing him to act in the verbally probing way that he was. I was scared if he moved even the slightest distance towards me, and if ever he used the name 'Becky' I was totally petrified.

Sometimes I would be locked up within myself for over an hour, and each time I thought it would never stop – I would be stuck like that for ever and taken away. The abuse did not feature anywhere in my conscious thoughts, and I had never told Stephen about it. Strange as it now seems, it did not seem to be as major an issue as the panic attacks.

I would do anything to avoid an attack. I discovered that if I messed around and joked I could avoid the inner pain that led into panic. It helped if I counted the various patterns on the carpet, or the dots on the wallpaper – and anything that stopped me looking at him, or being aware of him looking at me. If I was in a panic and he came towards me, I struck out at him and tried to make myself as small as I could so that he could not harm me.

Poor Stephen! What a way to start your pastoral counselling. Therefore it was hardly surprising that after about a year Stephen decided that we were not making enough progress. I found this extremely upsetting, because I felt he was saying I was not making enough effort. He suggested that he went with Fraser to see a Christian counsellor for further advice. They did this, and then I was given an appointment to visit the same female counsellor.

This was the first time I had been faced with a woman who was prepared to discuss all the issues. I desperately wanted help, and when I talked with her I did not feel any feelings of panic at all. I could look at her directly, and did not find her threatening. I was disappointed, though, that she never once mentioned God or my faith despite being a Christian counsellor. It mattered to me that she took an openly Christian perspective on healing.

When she had finished talking with me, she told Stephen that she felt I needed in-depth psychotherapy. Since she could not get me to talk about any of the issues that made me panic, she concluded that the problems must be extremely deep. She felt I needed a more qualified therapist than herself. She did not know of a Christian psychotherapist in the area, but said she would give us a list of reputable people in the city nearest our home.

There were two main problems, as I saw it: first, I did not feel I could respect this counsellor or her judgement based on the limited time we had spent together, and second, I did not have the time or the money to go for professional help. It was fine for her to pontificate on my needs, but in the circumstances what she suggested was unobtainable. In retrospect, her advice was probably good, but I could not take it. Had Stephen known more, he might have encouraged me more strongly to take that step. By this time, though, I was three months' pregnant with our second child, so I went to my GP to ask her advice. She felt that psychotherapy was a waste of time, which was exactly what I wanted to hear, so I told Stephen that I would not be going.

I regret now that I backed off at that point from receiving the help that could have made so much difference a lot earlier. I obviously did not understand the extent of the damage or the amount of support I was going to need, or I would not have run away from the necessary professional help. I still thought I was making good progress with Stephen and could not see the need for any other intervention.

Stephen felt uneasy about the future, but the agreement was reached that he would continue to see me, then review my progress in a year's time, when the baby would be six months old. I hoped that by then he would have forgotten all about the idea of professional help, so happily agreed to the review.

Stephen then set out pratical ways to try to make me change the way I was behaving. He encouraged me to take more effort in the way I dressed, and he tried to help me make myself look at people even when I felt threatened. He even tried to get me to resume hobbies I had long neglected in an attempt to get me to focus on myself and my needs. He made me talk about myself in more positive ways, and challenged me on how I saw situations, and by talking helped me to see that there were other perspectives. He tried to teach me to say 'no' to situations that were too demanding, whereas before I said 'yes' to everyone. He also sought to help me lower the mask I had used to cover myself, and encouraged every feeble attempt I made at sharing my vulnerability with others in the church, instead of keeping up the 'Superwoman' image that I had sought to perpetuate. Stephen worked alongside me, and used all that had happened in the fortnight between counselling sessions to move me towards healing. He certainly had a major struggle on his hands, because I still wanted to work so hard at everything. I had almost learned to be comfortable with my present lifestyle, and change was not going to come easily to me.

Our first daughter, Christine, was born not long after I had resumed my counselling with Stephen. The pregnancy had been difficult, for apart from the counselling and the inner turmoil I was experiencing I had felt ill throughout. All the time I felt as if it was the day after a bout of flu, and found it hard to look after Samuel, who was now a typically stroppy toddler, *and* be pregnant!

Peter had taken a more demanding job in an attempt to get his brain fully functional, and although it seemed like a good idea, it meant I saw less of him. He was gradually improving, but it was to be about another five years before I could honestly say that, apart from his poor memory, he was back to the man he had been before the accident. He was still unable to help me at all with anything emotional. However, he was excellent in realising this limitation, and so was very supportive of my going to see Stephen. He was just very glad that there was someone who I could get help from, and he did not seem threatened by the fact that it wasn't him. He looked after the children or prepared meals, so I had time to go for counselling.

Most of the time life was good, and it would be wrong to get the impression that counselling took up all my time and attention. Although life was very hectic, it was also lots of fun. I found it easier to cope with two children rather than one, in the respect that they were more demanding and therefore I found it more fulfilling. Peter and I took them everywhere. We were always going out, and we had endless picnics and games. Peter adored the children, and felt so much more pleasure when Christine was born than when Samuel arrived. He cried when she was born, and the tears meant such a lot to me – because I knew he was beginning to feel emotions again.

Most of the time, our house was full of people, and we even had a young couple living with us for a while. We often had people to stay the weekend because they needed a break. I continued to be busy with every activity in the church, and even though I now had two young children, I still considered it to be my job to visit anyone and everyone who was ill. I made little personal allowance for my own needs, or the demands that counselling made. I carried on regardless.

Stephen continued with my counselling, although it became less frequent after Christine's arrival. I did seem to be making progress, albeit very gradual. We had one comparatively easy year, and then I became pregnant again and the next problem arose.

12

Samuel was three and Christine had just had her first birthday when I became pregnant for the third time. Peter and I had planned it, so we were quite happy. We had always wanted a large family, as close together in age as possible. Some people in the church indicated that they thought that we were highly irresponsible. One older lady even came with her friend and offered us advice on contraception, since they could not imagine we had actually planned things this way! She suggested that we use the same method that she and her husband had used. I could not resist asking her what that was, and barely managed to suppress hysterical laughter when she whispered, 'I always jumped out of bed as soon as we had "done it" and it always worked for us.' I tried to explain that we did not lack knowledge of contraception and that all our babies had been planned, but she could hardly countenance that as a possibility.

Logically, I suppose it might have seemed sensible to wait, in view of the fact that I was still in such an emotional mess. However, both of us adored children, and we were so grateful that we had been able to have them. In spite of all the difficulties we had experienced in the last few years, our children were such a delight to us – even though they were very hard work.

Unfortunately, I had not allowed for the fact that my body could not take the strain of another child so quickly, and found I was in agony. The pain was acute and everywhere, so at first I was taken into hospital with suspected appendicitis, then I was told I had a problem with my lower spine. I was wrongly told that if I did not rest I might lose the baby. I was in such acute pain I could hardly do anything else anyway. It was terrible – no one could say how long it would go on for, nor did people seem to appreciate the degree of pain I was in.

I felt desperate, and could not physically care for our two young children. People in the church were marvellous, though, and organised rotas to help us out. In the end it turned out that I was in pain for the whole of the pregnancy. How I hated every minute of it. I don't think that the pain was the worst part either – I found it dreadful having to be so still, so helpless. I was unable to be in control for nearly seven months, and found myself feeling very vulnerable to whoever was around. It is hard for anyone to think straight when in acute pain, and I was no exception. I felt so angry with God. We had prayed for each child, and I felt he had let me down in allowing this pain and sickness.

However, I managed to keep up the counselling, since Stephen agreed to come to our house, but it was very difficult. The counselling centred mainly on coping with the day-to-day situation, for I had too much time to think, and I was afraid of damaging the child if I overdid things physically. I could no longer bake or go out, and was grounded at the mercy of everyone else.

Although I was a bad patient, a good side-effect was that Peter took more responsibility, caring for me in a way he had not had the chance to do since his accident, and the balance was restored a little more. Also, I found more time to talk with God and pray. I couldn't go to church often, so found that the times of worshipping on my own were very precious. On the bad days I would tell God just how mad I was at him. I asked him to tell me the areas in my life that needed dealing with so that I could sort them out and get on with my life. I prayed and prayed for the pain to go. The only answer I ever seemed to get was one phrase, and it was not the one that I wanted to hear: 'Be still and know that I am God.' How I longed to be able to do that!

Sarah arrived at the end of what seemed to me to have been the longest pregnancy on record. If I had found life difficult with two children, it was bordering on the impossible with three! However, I was just so relieved to be in action again that I set about getting back to my previous activities, and tried to work at repaying all the people for their kindnesses over the previous months. I know it was an impossible task, but I was desperate to show everyone I was fine. I did feel a lot stronger in myself emotionally, but I certainly wasn't going to wait around for the improvement to show gradually.

It was good to be back at church, and sometimes I would feel that God had spoken to me in a special way. I still felt deep down that my life was like a desert, but I didn't feel I could admit that to anyone – on the surface, everything was blossoming. It seemed to me that my life was an arid wasteland with only occasional places for feeling alive and whole. I had to learn then, as I have had to learn since, that God meets us in our desert experiences, just as much as he does when things are going well. I found that very difficult – I wanted God to be close only when things were fine. I hated him, or his children, reaching out to me when things were bad. This is what I wrote on one occasion when I really felt close to God. Although it was a rare experience for me, it was very precious.

Sabbath Manna
I murmured in my hungry heart against so many things,
as walking into church with façade so strong,
struggling,
hiding feeling deep.
I smiled,
but underneath there was no calm,
just angry tossing sea,
and screaming, I could not find God in me,
    or even glimpse him anywhere.
How could I praise him with any tiny part of
    hypocritical me,
for all pervasive bitterness and fear I had allowed to
canker conquer me?
So thus consumed within, by manna tightly held for
    many years,

I found my hand totally destroyed by worms which had
    eaten all which had
once been God's provision-peace.
I thought I stood looking all around,
but all I saw was me.
No more.
And hating that, I could not lift my head and perceive him
    anywhere,
or even any reality, however scarce.
I dared not feel 'the wind that could blow healthily, my
    sickness to heal',
but only felt the vacuum, dustless static air
    doubt dead in me.
I flattered God with my mouth, and I too lied with subtle
    tongue.

But he remembered I was flesh, a breeze, just blowing
    for a while not to come again,
and he knew my murmurings were against him.
Noiselessly I saw amidst the dry and sandy desert of
    myself the pure
and wholesome manna, softly, almost imperceptibly
fall,
But as I knelt down to pick some up with hungry
    craving soul,
I found my hands were all destroyed, and no small
    morsel could I hold
And, as I turned to shout at him, who had so cruelly
    taunting sent me blessing
knowing that I could not receive it, I felt his hands upon
    my lips.
With his touch he stopped my shouting screaming
    tongue.
Gently as though suckling child he succour-fed me with a
    pierced hand.
Until at last satisfied I dared to look just feelingly at
    himself.

But he was gone and all I could perceive was manna.
Yet when my tear-filled eyes looked down again with
    aching void,
expecting death, I didn't see the scorching, dying
    sand, or me.
I only saw the manna fresh.
So kneeling down I picked it gently with my whole hands.
And while I fed, my striving, smiling self stopped
    struggling.
There was no foe, no fear, no strife
Lying down I did not need to fight,
but slept in that day's soft snow manna bread.

Things were still not ideal, but I did feel there had been some improvement. In fact, when Stephen and Lois announced they were going to leave our church for another pastorate I was almost relieved. I knew that we would miss them as friends, but I felt I should be able to cope without all the counselling support. I hated counselling – no one else seemed to need it, so I felt a failure and wanted to be independent. I loathed the feeling that someone else had an element of control in my life, and I was fed up with so much self-examination. I wanted to put it all behind me and get on with living.

At this time we were very short of money, so I was doing private tuition at home for a few hours a week. I was now running the expanding daytime Bible study group, and I had three children under school age to entertain and care for all day. I still tried to visit sick and lonely people in the evenings. Ironically, I even had a few people who came to me for help and support during difficult times in their lives. I had given out such a strong image that people turned to *me* for help! Our house continued to be an open place for anyone, and most meals were shared with someone who had a problem.

I was sure I had dealt with all the issues in my life, but Stephen knew that I had not dealt with everything. As our time together drew to an end, he went along with my conviction that I was healed, but inwardly he felt uncertain about my future. He has said since that he knew we had somehow never got to the central issues, but didn't know what to do about it.

So Stephen and Lois left, and Peter and I carried on getting busier and busier. I still felt very depressed at times, but put this down to exhaustion rather than inner turmoil. In the daytime my house was always a hive of activity. Other mums who were lonely would come round as they knew I loved their company, and I tried to organise it so someone was always there. I tried to convince myself that I was fine alone, but in reality I was terrified and still felt hunted inside. I made sure I avoided any situations where people might ask me how I really was, so the panics got less and less. The reality was that I had not changed the issues at all – I had merely learned to sidestep them.

Ironically, away from all the counselling, the memory of my sexual abuse started to return. I wanted it to go away, but having successfully avoided it for so long I knew I had to face it sometime. I did not have a counsellor to discuss it with, and anyway I wanted to sort it out myself. Peter and I had not mentioned it since early in our marriage. I simply wanted to forget it, and Peter had no memory of it at all since his accident. Our sexual life was less than ideal, but since the previous four years had been spent with me either pregnant or breastfeeding, I always had a good explanation as to why I was not enthusiastic about sex.

I decided to pray about the abuse. This in itself was a breakthrough as far as I was concerned, since I had never mentioned it to God before. So I knelt down to pray, and asked God to make me feel better inside. I did not hear an audible voice, but I had a deep inner knowing that God had said, 'Go and forgive him.' This was certainly not what I wanted to hear. I was sure the Lord could not actually mean me to go in person – that would be unthinkable. So I told the Lord that I honestly forgave Mr Sutherland for all he had done to me and that, I felt, was the end of it.

Yet somewhere deep within me I knew that that wasn't enough. It was easy in the comfort of my own home to forgive the man, but how did I know if I meant it? Was the forgiveness worth it if I couldn't actually do it face to face, I wondered? In any case, the Lord had clearly told me to *go* and forgive him.

I didn't know where to begin, and I started to sob before God. I could not possibly go and see Mr Sutherland. What would I say? Where would I start? How could I honestly forgive him? When I was faced with the possibility of seeing him face to face, I had to think whether I really did want to forgive him, for it was slowly beginning to dawn on me that some of my problems were caused by him – although I had no idea then just how many. How could I walk into his life again after twenty years and pronounce that I had forgiven him? What difference would it make to either of us?

I tried to pray, and desperately hoped for a different answer. The childish heart in me wanted this man to know that Jesus had forgiven him; I wanted to go to him as an adult and tell him what I had failed to convey to him all those years before. I really wanted something good to come out of this awful situation. I still felt responsible for the events, and I wanted to put it right now. I started to feel very scared that he would have died by now, and that I wouldn't have the chance to see him. I was also frightened that if I actually saw him I would want to hurt him, and that everything would go drastically wrong.

The solution I had been given in prayer was not the simple, quick, healing one I had hoped for, and I began to wish that I had never prayed about the subject in the first place. Yet I felt so strongly that it was the right thing to do. I told Peter, and we started to plan our visit.

13

Peter was very supportive of the decision I had made, and I was touched that he was prepared to come with me. I wanted him to meet the man he had only been able to imagine until then. I hoped this would mean that we could share more fully, and that maybe this visit would heal some of our difficulties. Nine years had passed since I had first told Peter, and now, for the first time, I wanted to go further.

Mr Sutherland no longer worked in the woodshed, of course, and by the time I visited him he was eighty-four years old. One part of me so much wanted him to be alive, although another part hoped he was dead so that I wouldn't have to go through with the ordeal of seeing him again.

This was the first time I had been to his sister's house since the occasion twenty years before, when Lizzie and I had been so concerned about his health. Peter and I took baby Sarah with us. I had no idea what to expect, and felt very nervous. I tentatively knocked on the door.

We heard shuffling behind the door, and I knew it was Mr Sutherland. He opened the door slowly and blinked at the sunshine. He was a short man: whereas as a child I had always looked up to him, now I was much taller than he was. I was surprised because I thought he would look very different, but he was exactly the same as I remembered him. He was obviously quite deaf, and we ended up shouting at him to get him to understand.

'I'm Rebecca,' I said. 'Do you remember me?'

He stared blankly at us.

I had forgotten that I had changed my name since I had seen him last. He was bent over and shuffled round, looking first at the floor and then at me.

'Remember?' I tried again. 'Remember Rebecca? I was the little girl who came to see you.'

He looked up at me, straight into my eyes, and then a look of recognition spread across his old and wrinkled face. He broke into a big smile.

'Becky, little Becky with those blue eyes! I remember you.'

Then suddenly, the implication of who I was struck him, and he became agitated and frightened. He looked abruptly at Peter. 'What do you want?' It hadn't occurred to me before that he would be scared of us. I assured him we did not mean him any harm – we were visiting as friends. He stood aside and gestured for us to go in.

The sight that met our eyes was appalling. There was mess everywhere, and he was obviously living the life of a virtual recluse. All round the room were half-eaten bits of food and the smell was terrible. In fact, he smelt the same as before, but the pervading smell of the freshly sawn wood was missing.

He had the same unhappy appearance as he had the first time I met him. His face had not changed – he was still wrinkled and pink, his thin lips dribbling saliva. His eyes still had that moist, reddish look, and his hands were still chubby, but not so cracked. His clothes didn't fit him, and were just as filthy as they had been before.

Awkwardly, we all sat down. Peter held Sarah close to him, and left me free to talk to Mr Sutherland.

I was amazed to find that in that instant God had given me the ability to forgive. I honestly felt no hatred or anger for this old man who sat opposite me. And what had begun as a vague hope that he would become a Christian now turned into an overwhelming desire for this to be so.

'Mr Sutherland,' I began rather stiffly, 'I have come because I want to tell you that I forgive you for what you did to me all those years ago.' The tears flowed silently and swiftly down my face. 'It's not easy to forgive you – I can only do it because I love Jesus. I want to tell you about him and what he means to me.'

The old man's face suddenly lit up, and I could hardly believe his words when he broke in with, 'I was only in prison for a month. I was discharged early on medical grounds because they said I was mentally ill, and that prison was not the right place for me. In that month I was inside, I became a Christian.' Peter and I were beside ourselves with joy, because this had mattered to us enormously. It wasn't so much that God had got me there for Mr Sutherland to hear *me*, but rather that I could hear *him*!

He then went on to talk about what he had done to us all. He said that he never knew why he did what he did, and that he had never done it before or since. I have no way of knowing if that was the truth, but I wanted to believe it was true. All I have since found out about abuse leads me now to doubt it. He then asked me if he had harmed me in any way.

My one regret about this time together was that I didn't say, 'Yes, you did harm me. You harmed me terribly, and I still forgive you.' I thought then that forgiveness meant forgetting the sin, but how wrong I was. I should have faced him with as much of the damage as I knew and then still forgiven him. As it was, when I looked at the pathetic figure before me, I said, 'No, it's all right.'

Then he slowly turned to Peter and asked, 'Have I spoiled things for you?' It seemed that by actually asking such questions he had shown that he now had a far greater understanding of the extent of the damage done by abuse, and it was a welcome far cry from the man who had long before told me he was doing it for my pleasure.

Peter made the same mistake that I had, and said that everything was fine. The old man then said: 'You must be a very special man to come here like this.' He then reached out towards me and said that he was very sorry for what he had done, and we hugged each other. All of us were in tears by now, except for Sarah who was oblivious to what was going on. It was a very beautiful and healing hug. There was nothing secret about it. Peter was there, and was a part of it. I felt in his holding me and my holding him that I knew I had forgiven him for all he had done wrong. I felt the overwhelming love of Jesus just pouring through me. It was a very special moment.

Suddenly it was all over, and there was nothing more to say. I kissed him goodbye and we left, with both Peter and I feeling very glad that we had visited him. Now that Peter had seen Mr Sutherland for himself, he seemed to understand far better how I could have got myself into such a mess in my attempts to help him. Mr Sutherland didn't look like someone who would harm anyone – in fact, he looked gentle and kind, and desperately in need of love and care.

As events turned out, I was so glad that I had acted promptly on what God had told me to do, for less than two years later, when I returned to see how he was, he was no longer there. Neighbours said that he had gone into a home and they thought he had since died.

I wish that this was the end of the book. It would be so convenient if I could write that this experience was the end of my pain, the solving of all my problems. Certainly, that was how I had anticipated things would be. If I had been receiving outside help at this time, maybe someone would have enabled me to see that this experience was not meant to be the end of my healing, but as a place for me to start. It had cost me so dearly to visit Mr Sutherland, that I honestly didn't think there was anything more to be done. Since I had faced him in the way that I had, I might have had a good foundation for starting my healing. Instead, I used the whole experience to close down this area of my life yet again. I had forgiven Mr Sutherland, and that, I thought, was the end of it all.

For the next four years I denied every negative thought that came into my head about the situation, and I decided it was Satan trying to get me to lose the power of God's forgiveness. The truth was that I could not begin to face the real extent of the damage that Mr Sutherland had caused. I did not tell anyone about the visit, and locked all my feelings up again as I had learned to do so well for many years.

By this time, I felt as if I had changed a lot, and in the year that followed I did not have much time for introspection for I got a teaching job that took up four hours a week. This looked like madness to the outside world, but in reality it was a very well-paid hobby! I viewed the teaching as more of an outing than anything else – I was just so glad to get out and leave the little ones behind just for a while. It was great to get back to doing something I enjoyed so much. I was teaching mature students as well, and loved their adult company. It was so good to talk about something other than nappies and sleepless nights!

I was also having weekly treatment for my back, so that for any future pregnancy I would not experience the same problems I had with Sarah. It might seem strange that Peter and I were so set on having still more children. The regrets I have about the past are many, but neither of us has ever regretted having had five children. Sometimes it seems really amazing that we were able to have children in spite of all the problems. They have been such a wonderful gift to us, although many times, in the middle of the night, we haven't felt quite so spiritual about the situation! I would be so sad now if I thought we would have had more children had I not been abused. That would have been a greater regret than the slowness of healing I experienced – partly because the children kept arriving!

However, I did not enjoy being pregnant – I did not look or feel like other women seemed to. I felt ghastly the whole time, tired and sick, and just longed for it to be over. Also, when I am pregnant I am not able to think straight, and everything takes more effort. On the plus side, I have always had easy births, and as soon as the baby is born I feel fine. So I suppose I should be thankful for that!

We planned our fourth baby, and decided to ignore the shocked reactions we knew we would get from some people in the church. This pregnancy was the easiest of them all. I was able to swim and exercise throughout, and although I still felt ill, it was as nothing compared to being on bed-rest.

During this particular year I had started a daytime study club. Apart from our discussions, I felt we should all be sharing things a lot more. We shared children's clothes easily enough, but, if we were honest, the mothers needed new clothes more than the children did! Hence, I started a small swap table in my house. People put things they didn't want on the table and anyone who came to the house could take anything off it. It seemed a small gesture, and hardly worth mentioning, but for the way it was to develop in the next few years.

My life continued to be as hectic as ever throughout this fourth pregnancy, and Matthew was born in the middle of a quiet October night. By this time, we felt things were definitely improving. I might have escaped any further counselling, and could still have been living in my deluded state now, were it not for the fact that I became severely depressed after Matthew's birth. I will never know if this was hormonally caused, or if it was the direct result of all the build-up of previous years. Whatever the reason, it was real enough. I could not face anything or anyone. I wanted to cry all the time, and could not believe we had planned all the children. I simply felt I could not cope with them. Nothing had improved: I was back where I had been during the years before. I hated myself. I could not bear to be living in my body. Once again, I was unable to look at others, and all the feelings I had hidden for so long just rushed back to the surface. This time, though, I had four children under six to look after as well.

By now we had a new pastor at the church, John, who arrived with Margaret his wife. I had welcomed them with the same enthusiasm I had given the previous minister, and I was desperate this time to be the 'successful and supportive' church member I had tried to be for so many years. It wasn't long, though, before I could hide the depression no longer. My friends knew how bad things were, and John suggested that I went for a chat with him. I did not relish the prospect. I felt so low that I thought counselling was a complete waste of time. I felt that I had had enough counselling to last me a lifetime, and did not want any more, but I was so desperate that I had no alternative but to go and see him.

14

I recognised that I needed help, but just hoped that the new pastor and his wife could sort things out quickly so that I could get on with life. At first the chats we had were fairly general, and I felt we were getting nowhere. I told John about the panic attacks, depression, Peter's accident, and my feelings of worthlessness, which by this time bordered on self-hatred. I even mentioned to John that I had been abused as a child.

Unfortunately John had little knowledge of abuse. I told him the facts, but added that I had been to see the abuser and forgiven him face to face. Ironically, this was the only area in my life that I considered to be sorted out! John came to the same conclusion, and decided to tackle the other areas that he thought needed dealing with. How much time and pain we would all have been spared if we had both understood that the abuse was the underlying cause of all the other issues.

After about three sessions of counselling, John pronounced that he thought there were three main areas of my life that needed dealing with. I was relieved at this diagnosis – I felt so useless that I was convinced there were *hundreds* of areas!

'What areas are they?' I asked tentatively.

'Well, I think mainly you have a wrong view of God, a wrong view of yourself, and a wrong view of other people.'

I was stunned. It may have been only *three* areas, but it didn't leave a lot else! However, John was correct in his assessment of me: I was not seeing *anything* straight. When we started to examine how I felt about each of these areas, I began to realise that they were all interrelated. I felt God was out to judge me and condemn me, and that he only wanted me if I could please him and do all the right things. I felt terrible about myself, as I could never make the grade and, however hard I worked, I always failed. I could not trust other people, because I felt they would only love me on condition that I was good to them. I was too scared to face up to the possibility or demands of unconditional love from God or other people. It is not surprising that John felt he already had enough to deal with, just as Stephen had done. He did not attempt to look any further back for the cause of such a distorted viewpoint.

I soon became very angry with John's diagnosis. If what he said was correct, he could be counselling me for the rest of my life – *everything* about me was wrong! He said that he felt the best way to proceed was to go step by step, dealing with the parts of each issue as they arose, and as God revealed them to us. However, it all sounded so slow, and I needed healing fast! Patience has never been one of my virtues, so I asked John why everything had to be so slow. Why couldn't we just ask God to show us everything in one go, and deal with it all at once? It might be drastic, but I didn't feel I was able to cope with any more tedious and painful counselling. John gently explained that it was a bit like a tunnel, and my way was blocked because of a lot of stones in the way. We needed to look at each stone and move it to the side, he explained.

'Why can't we just get dynamite and explode them?' I asked impatiently.

'Because the person on the other side might get damaged, and she is too precious for that,' came the reply.

I knew at this point that I had met my match. John seemed to know what he was doing, and I had to trust him as far as I was able. I didn't want to, but I had little option. Margaret always sat with us for the counselling sessions, and that was very helpful. I didn't know why at the time, but I felt so much safer if there was a woman in the room. She said little, but I think her presence made the subsequent revealing of the abuse possible.

The following year was spent yet again going over various aspects of my life that were in a mess. When I had told John about the panic attacks, he had nodded understandingly. However, when the first attack came, he was quite unprepared. I cannot now remember the question he had asked – all I know was that terror was rising within me. I had thought that I was free of these attacks, and I was very angry and frightened that John had been able to trigger one off. I could not speak to him, and found again that I couldn't even move. I was terrified because I knew what was happening, but could do nothing to stop it. I was scared John would become angry, and throw me out or hurt me. He tried to carry on talking, but it got worse and worse and he could see I was shaking violently. When he and Margaret tried to come towards me to hold me, I went completely wild. I hit out with all the strength I had and tried to push them away. At the same time, I attempted to curl up even further and lose myself in the chair. I wanted to scream and shout. The anger I felt was so intense that, however violently I moved, it was not an adequate expression of it. Although part of me knew that John was trying to help, I hated him with my whole being. I didn't know what he had said that had set it off, but I felt he had done it all on purpose. Eventually, John sat down and talked quietly. He said that he didn't understand what was happening, but that God would help us to sort it out.

Gradually, I began to calm down and the shaking subsided. I still couldn't look at either of them, but I could begin to speak. Slowly, John tried to take me back to the sentences he had said that had triggered off the panic attack. At last I felt progress was being made. Up until now, the panic attacks had served the purpose of diverting counsellors away from the real issues. Now, it seems, I had to face them. This was a different style of counselling to anything I had known before. Every time John was stuck, he asked God to help us through the next stage.

Although this did ultimately prove helpful, I found it very difficult. It felt as if I was having to lose control and let God lead to get anything sorted out, and I hated that. Often John would pray and I would add a grudging 'Amen', but I never could figure out how on earth God could break into this situation and change me. Sometimes as we prayed, John would feel that God told him which direction we should go in. At other times, I would see a picture or something that would move us on. Each time we asked, God did answer, but not always in the way we thought.

Overall, I was still angry that I was back in a counselling situation and hated going. I always resolved that I would try and be as open as I could to John's and Margaret's help and to God's healing, but by the time I got there and had knocked on the door, I always felt scared. I was frightened of what they might uncover. On the one hand, I wanted God to heal me, but at the same time I was terrified that he might! On some occasions I panicked, sometimes I didn't. In some sessions I felt God was very close, and began to feel I was really being healed. At other times, I despaired completely. I thought I would never be any different.

Sometimes I could not face John and Margaret at all, and then I would resort to a letter to explain how I felt. John had set clear guidelines, and I knew I could not see him between booked counselling sessions. This in fact proved to be helpful. They lived very close to us, and it would have been easy to run to them every time there was a problem. John kept all my letters, and returned them to me to read for the purpose of writing this book, so that I could remember more clearly how things really were at the time.

When I re-read the following letter, I realised just how depressed I had been, and how the whole of my family life was affected. Despite this, I was still very busy in the church, and as determined as ever to keep going in spite of counselling. It also shows that I had completely abandoned any hope of being seen as anything less than 'The Church Problem'!

Dear John and Margaret,
It might seem really silly to be writing to you like this, but I can't think what else to do. I am just trying to sort out something in my own head, and I am going round in circles on it. I thought I would get it on to paper and sort it out. I might not actually send the letter to you anyway. At the moment, I have a migraine brewing, and I feel completely exhausted. Things were going really well over the last

week. I keep teetering on the edge of saying I need to chat to you before next Wednesday, but I am grimly determined to hang on until then, come what may. I am really cross at myself that I just cannot cope. I wish that I could envisage a time when things will be different, but right now I am not so sure. It is so silly, I have had some good times this week, and had loads of fun.

Yesterday I was so mad that I couldn't even last one and a half hours on my own without needing to ring someone. It sounded dreadfully pathetic. I struggled inside to keep going, and all the while that awful feeling just got worse and worse. As soon as people are with me I am OK again. That feels like living such a lie. It can also be very manipulative. I can easily use people just to keep me going.

Sometimes I try and think hard about all we have discussed and sometimes I think that we have got somewhere. Then I find myself not coping and it all seems to go.

Well, the headache is still there, but at least my typing is improving! I wish that I could cry and cry right now, but I just don't know what for. This is the first time that I have sat down and tried to concentrate my thoughts since last Wednesday. It is so hectic the rest of the time. I am going a bomb on trying to improve 'the image', but inside it does not feel any better. Bible Study was hard this morning. The other women seemed very 'got-it-together', and seemingly find it a lot less of a battle than I do. I felt really unhealed and not at all victorious.

The children have been a real strain today. I have no space for them. I can't be doing the Lord's work right if at the end of the day I am out of space for the children. I really shouted at Samuel tonight, and it wasn't fair. I had to apologise to the sobbing wreck at prayer time tonight. Isn't it awful that you feel as though any good you might have done is undone in one small incident, and that is the only one that they are never going to forget! Even little Matthew was frightened. Sometimes I get frightened at myself, and then I just feel so wretched. I remember my mum going crazy sometimes and I was so scared. I can understand it so much better now, but I don't want to be the same as her in this respect. I just can't get the gradual side of all this sorting out. It is so slow. It wouldn't be as bad if I thought it was all going to be sorted out next Wednesday. I know that it isn't. I dread the thought of chatting again, and yet I cannot wait to chat. I will explode if I don't get something out of my system, but I don't even know what it is. Talking just lets enough steam out to keep the pressure cooker from bursting, and yet it doesn't get the head turned off from underneath. So nothing changes, does it?

Well, I guess this is being 'overdrawn' time. I don't know exactly what I have overdone, but physically I have done too much or I would not have been so tired emotionally. I have misjudged it all because I am so screwed up. I am not sure where to go from here. I guess a good night's sleep could help a heap. I am so tired of living with me. I wish that I was someone less exhausting, that I was more relaxed to be with, much less intense, bordering on the lazy. I would love to be someone who just loves lolling around doing nothing, with no one else near. It would be a lot easier.

I shall discuss this letter with Peter and he can decide whether I let you glimpse these self-centred meanderings. Please don't comment on all above. I probably won't feel like it for long anyway. Just another week seems to be a long time until we chat, and this seemed like a good in-between.

I hope that you and Margaret are all right.

See you sometime.

Love Rebecca

Counselling was a tremendous strain on all the family. I only told a few people that I was seeing John, as I was deeply ashamed that I needed such help. If I was a better person, I thought, I would have managed without it. I wrote the days I was seeing him in coded messages on the calendar, so that others seeing it on the wall would not know what I was doing.

I tried to carry on as normally as possible in front of everyone else. As always, this meant that I had to be perpetually busy. With four small children it was impossible to get out of the house every time I felt frightened at being alone. It seems strange that the children didn't stop that feeling of aloneness, but I needed adults around.

The only way I could handle the rising fear was to start cooking. On bad days I would go shopping in the morning and buy as many ingredients as we could possibly afford and cook main meals all day. By the time Peter came home, the kitchen would look horrendous – although cooking relaxed me, clearing up didn't! The freezer would be full to bursting and the children would be fractious because they hadn't had enough attention – but at least *I* felt better!

If the freezer was over-full, I would bake endless cakes and give them away to anyone or any function that needed them. Cooking was like the Christian alternative to drinking or smoking for me! I guess it was less harmful, but it was quite excessive. I was still teaching, and those times were oases in my week. I loved to go to work and lose myself for a while. All the while, some people at church still held on to my 'Superwoman' image, and I was too scared to tell them otherwise.

I had been seeing John for about a year when I came across a booklet produced by the local authority about children and abuse. At the end of the booklet it said that many people coming to terms with sexual abuse in their past could suffer problems in their sexual relationships as adults. As I read this booklet, I felt that someone had shown me at last where the key was, and I read it over and over again. Our sexual relationship, although improved, could not be described as dynamic, and we were still struggling between Peter's normal enthusiasm and my marked indifference.

I did not realise then what a tiny tip of the iceberg I was looking at. I was so excited about the booklet that I decided to show it to John the very next time I saw him, even if it was a social visit. I don't know what I expected him to say, but it was the first admission I had made to anyone that Peter and I were still having sexual problems. John calmly said that what I had read was true, then I talked a little bit about Peter and me – just enough for him to realise that all was not well. John then suggested that the next time we met we should talk about the abuse.

At last I felt I had begun to get on to the right road. I had denied what had happened to me for twenty-five years, but finally I had decided to face it properly. I had to acknowledge that, even though I had been to see Mr Sutherland, and even though I had forgiven him as best I knew how, it was not enough. It had taken me a year of counselling with John and Margaret to feel I could trust them enough with the information that I had been abused and was damaged by it. I didn't realise that digging deeper was to be like pulling the pin out of a hand grenade. Once I started to deal with the abuse it was like an explosion – nothing could ever put the pieces back into hiding again.

15

I started to talk about the abuse just before the summer holidays, so the only session I had before a long break was a very general one. John said that abuse did have serious consequences, and that perhaps it might explain some of the other aspects of my life that were difficult for me. I told him the broad outline of what had happened, and he said that we would look at things more closely when I returned from holiday.

I didn't know why, but the thought of dealing in detail with the abuse filled me with terror. I so wanted to be healed, but I still could not believe that something that had happened to me so many years before could honestly make much difference at all. I felt as if I was trying to find something in the past to explain what I felt to be immature and appalling behaviour in the present. What I really thought was that I was simply a bad person, and that I should try to be a better one. I had not appreciated the far-reaching and devastating consequences of abuse.

That summer, we were going on holiday to a remote Scottish village. A friend had kindly lent us his house for three weeks, and it seemed too good an opportunity to pass by. If I had been honest, there was nowhere in the world that I would less have liked to go. I desperately needed people and the thought of being a long way away with no one else around was my idea of a nightmare rather than a holiday. However, with no real finances to provide an alternative, we set off with the children.

The concept of a 'holiday' had long since disappeared with the arrival of our first child. Going away with children is sheer hard work. It is enjoyable, it is part of being a family, it is all those things we believe are good, but it is not a 'holiday'! Apart from the complete nightmare of packing up clothes when there isn't any space in the car because we have so many children, there is the endlessly long journey to cope with.

When it comes to all this, I try to be very positive, and go into what Peter describes as 'teacher mode'. This means that I decide that we are going to learn as much as we possibly can from the experience. We spend the first hour or so talking about everything we see, then we all play games, working out the first letters of things, and talking about numbers, shapes, and sizes. After this, I have had enough of entertaining and educating, and just want the journey to be over with! The novelty of being cramped in the car and taking it in turns to breathe quickly wears off, the children start to rebel at being 'educated', and we just try to survive the rest of the journey.

By the time we stop for a lunch break, we can never find the place we want, the sandwiches are squashed, and we sit eating our picnic, bearing a closer resemblance to refugees than a happy family going on holiday! Doubtless, there will be many reading this who will identify with the experience!

To make matters worse, I feel more insecure than usual because I hate going away. I can't bear the feeling of being so unsettled and, unless I am in 'teacher mode', this means I am snappier and more restless than usual. Fortunately for the children, the more stressed I get, the calmer Peter becomes. By the time we arrive anywhere after a long journey, I am a nervous wreck and he is 'spaced out' – oblivious to everything!

When we finally got to Scotland on this occasion, it took me the first three days to unwind from the journey. In contrast, the children carried on regardless and had wonderful time. They are quite happy when they are left to play, and are expert at making up creative games and exploring.

After several days of short trips out exploring the country-side, we decided to visit the nearest main town. I pretended that the children needed to go, but it was really because I could not stand the space and the solitude for one minute longer.

We wandered around the shops – as best you can with four bored children under seven – and ended up in a Christian bookshop. I don't know why, but I hate going into Christian bookshops. So often there is an air of sanctified quietness and holiness, and while for the majority this may be a marvellous oasis, for a mother of young children it is a mild form of purgatory. The children seemed to be worse in there than anywhere else – they poked at everything, they wanted to spend their holiday money, and they were talking loudly and moving fast! The other people in the shop looked quietly contemplative, and I wanted to get out as quickly as I could.

Just at that moment, Peter came over to me with two books in his hands, and neither of us could believe the titles. One was called *Child Sexual Abuse: A Hope for Healing* and the other was about incest and was called *A Silence to be Broken*. Both titles filled me with excitement. One promised hope and the other offered the possibility that this dark secret would not be locked in me for ever.

I was so pleased to see these books in a Christian shop. I had never imagined that the experiences I had gone through could have happened to anyone else, and certainly it was not the sort of thing that I had even considered a Christian could suffer. As we got to the counter, I felt that the man behind it must have realised I had been abused. He took one look at me, and then suggested we might like to buy another book they stocked on the subject in a series entitled 'Hope'. The book was an autobiographical account and was called *When You've Been Abused*.

My excitement at finding these books was so immense that I let the children spend their money after all. Suddenly, I didn't care *what* they did! I felt that in my hands we had the key to the problem. I assumed that if I read the books I would get the help I needed: I could find out what other people had done, do the same, and all would be well. It would be as simple as that.

*   *   *

I couldn't wait for the children to go to bed that night, as I was desperate to read the books. Peter and I tucked the children in, and then each chose a book. Now this *really* felt like a holiday. At last we were by ourselves, no one was likely to ring and disturb us, and we had important books to read. Slowly, I began to relax.

I had hardly read even a page when I realised that these books were not the instant solution I had hoped for. I felt terribly despondent, and an almost physical pain welled up inside me as I read. I started to cry about the abuse for the first time. Slowly, I began to realise the way things fitted together, and that I was not going insane. Lots of other people had experienced abuse, it seemed, and it was such a relief to read about their experiences. No one in the books had experienced exactly the same events as me, but there were so many common threads that this meant that I was not alone.

Despite this sense of relief, I had never felt such an emotional upheaval when I had started to read any book before, and I did not know how to even begin to explain it to Peter. I looked across at him, and realised that he was feeling the same things. Our silence was only interpersed when one of us read out a sentence to the other.

My tears flowed faster, and I could hardly see the words. I read, for example, that some abused women had turned to prostitution and others had started stealing as a way of attracting attention to their need for help. Some had become anorexic or bulimic, and virtually everyone had suffered some kind of depression. The picture was so bleak, the effects of abuse so vast. The lack of trust that seemed to be a universal consequence of abuse had resulted in the failure of many marriages and poor relationships with children. For some, the effects of the depression had even led them to suicide.

The statistics in the books were alarming. One in four women had experienced abuse and one in twelve men. It appeared that women were not the only ones to be abused, and men were not the only abusers: women could abuse

and men were sometimes victims. The situation was so
complicated and ghastly. I sobbed and sobbed as I identified
with the pain of those writing. The panics and depression that
I experienced had seemed before to be so dreadful, but when
I realised what might have been, I wept with relief at the pain
I had been spared. I knew that I was happily married and that I
loved the children – things could have been so much worse.

I wanted to finish the book in one go, but just could not
cope with it. By now, we had been reading for over an hour.
I slowly closed the book, and looked at Peter. For the first
time in years I saw tears in his eyes, and we clung to one
another sobbing as we began to realise how much damage
Mr Sutherland had done to us both.

I woke up the next day with a feeling of heaviness, a kind
of grief. It was as if something in me had died. There was an
awful feeling of nameless, endless loss. There was no actual
death to acknowledge, yet it was as if one of our children
had died. The pain was immense, and I felt a kind of futile
searching for it to stop.

The children seemed to be in the way. I wanted to do
nothing else except be alone and cry; my mind was so full of
jumbled thoughts and I needed time to sort things out. Peter
took the children out for a walk in the morning, while I stayed
in bed, numbly crying. The tears wouldn't stop. I wasn't even
sure what exactly I was crying about, or why a few chapters
of a book had had such a devastating effect on me.

Somehow we got through the rest of the day, and then
in the evening we read again. Sometimes I read chapters
repeatedly as I tried to absorb the impact of them. We
spent the following evenings reading and crying together;
sometimes we prayed. We ached emotionally and physically.
In the daytime we would make an effort and take the children
out somewhere special. We were both determined that they
should not suffer, and we kept our inner pain from them.

The books helped us so much. For the first time, they gave
us an independent framework as a basis for our discussions.
Until then we had not been able to be specific about problems,
things that Peter found difficult about me, or areas that were

hard in our relationship. The more we read, the more the pieces of the jigsaw were slotting into place. Attitudes and feelings that had seemed to come from nowhere and be out of keeping with the rest of my character were being described by others who had been abused. I was neither bad nor mad, but I was severely damaged.

We discovered that sexual difficulties were highly likely for anyone who had been abused. I was not cold and unresponsive from my lack of desire for Peter, but because of what had happened to me as a child. By reading what someone else had written, I was able to tell Peter more easily how it felt for me. It was so painful reading and talking for the first time, but it was essential. My feelings about the abuser were so strong as I read, that I half feared he would walk into the room at any time. I had tried to forget him when I had gone to forgive him, but it was as if he had come alive as I unburied my deep memories of what had happened. Unfortunately, since I was reliving the experiences in such a vivid way, anything was enough to trigger off a reaction.

On one afternoon we took the children out for a walk to the nearby village. Apart from the feeling of grief that had never left me since I had first read the books, I was coping quite well and we were having a good time. Suddenly, we walked past a wood shop. In my adult mind I made no connection at all, and kept walking and chatting. Then I smelt the freshly sawn wood and saw, to my horror, that outside the shop there were bundles of wood for fires, the same as Mr Sutherland had made.

My response was immediate and terrible. I grabbed hold of Peter and told him that we had to get away as quickly as we could. The children were totally bewildered, and Peter couldn't reassure them as he didn't know what was going on either. Even I didn't know what was happening; I only knew I was terrified and had to escape to somewhere safe. I was breathless and shaking as we got the children into the car.

When we were safely home, I calmed down enough to begin to rationalise what had been happening. I had suddenly felt that Mr Sutherland was there with us, that he had followed us somehow, and that in a strange way I could never lose him. I felt hunted and watched and this terrified me.

As a child I had never been able to run away from him, but now as an adult faced with the same feelings, that was all I was able to do. I realised that all the time he was abusing me I could smell freshly sawn wood, and this had been the trigger. Until I started to deal with the abuse, the smell had not affected me, but now it made me feel physically sick.

We stayed at home quietly for the rest of the day, and I felt foolish as I tried to explain to the children why we had to hurry home. Obviously, I could not give them an adequate explanation – I was acting like the young girl had wanted to act. The response this time was to run and run and never go back, but it was now too late and my response was inappropriate.

16

I appreciate that when people look back on something, their memories can be coloured by their present experiences, and so give a distorted picture. Again, I am so glad that I wrote to John and Margaret from Scotland, because the letter gives me a marvellous insight into how things really were. The letter is exactly as I wrote it, but omitting those parts that aren't relevant to my story.

Dear John and Margaret,
I shall have to communicate with you or I shall burst. It has been a fortnight since we talked last, and I would have been seeing you tonight, so don't think that you are getting away with the quiet life! As usual, most of what I write is to help me to think things through rather than expecting an answer from you. It has taken all the time so far to stop feeling just exhausted. Neither of us had realised just how tired we were. We have got up late, and often in the day we have taken it in turns to look after the children while the other one sleeps. It sounds as if we are in our nineties! I would have thought that by now we would feel wonderful, but we don't. Peter is generally improved, but he has gone back to taking a lot more of his tablets. [Peter had needed tablets to control possible epilepsy following his motorbike accident.] He has been cutting down over the last few months, but perhaps he had been too drastic. That, coupled with the tiredness, produced the symptoms he has been experiencing. He still isn't 100 per cent. One problem is that, with the children, we can't get to stop at all. Even in the evenings we still have loads of jobs to do. I don't mean to sound miserable and it is loads easier than

at home, but this holiday is not exactly 'unrestricted leisure time'. I have never done so much ironing and washing. We have cut back on it as much as we can, but even with all the junk foods in the world there is heaps to do.

Emotionally I am all over the place. Sometimes I feel so relaxed I just can't believe it, other minutes I am so tearful and tense it is ridiculous! At times I feel that God is so close, and we are going to make it through, then I feel miles away from God, and as if I am getting nowhere. This holiday seems to give endless personal space, but I feel that in reality I would have more space in a rabbit hutch! Sometimes I am so homesick it is all I can do not to give up and come home. Then after a while I feel as if I could live here for ever. Overall, I do appreciate the life we have back home a lot more after living here. Our church drives me crazy at times, but here I would go completely mad. We both appreciate your ministry more than ever, but honestly the competition here is pretty dismal!

When I read the books on abuse I realised again just how blessed I am to have an excellent counsellor. I do trust you both and I think that I have gone a long way. When I read how some people have fared I actually feel very blessed! This, as you can see, is a good moment. I guess my frustration is how long and slow it all is. When I read the book I began to feel that it has been relatively quick in view of the damage that has been done. Margaret, it helped so much when you said last time that you were surprised how good things were in view of how bad the damage had been. I needed to hear you say that desperately. I keep saying it to myself, at the bad times especially. I felt quite 'got-it-together' at times when I read the book. Sometimes when I read the book it felt as if it was a completely open wound and no healing had taken place at all. Peter and I have talked ever such a lot more than we have done before. It is good that I can't run to you all the time. We both feel that we hardly knew what we were forgiving when we went to see Mr Sutherland. Peter summed it up really well. I asked him if knowing what we know now he would still have forgiven him. 'Yes, I would have,' he replied, 'but I guess I would have thumped him first and then forgiven him.' We are both so angry now, and I know we are working through that stage. The books make us really mad about the situation we are in because of him. I guess we need more grace. Tons more!

Next day.

How can I get the balance between being too introspective and not facing the past at all? Surely I am more than the sum of all that has happened to me, and I cannot hide behind the past as a way of showing myself. Yet, at the same time, can anyone really know me without understanding what has happened? Is it possible to be real without people knowing? I cannot wait for death to understand what has happened. I need some joy and peace about it now. Yes, I know that the latter is possible without the former, but that is so theoretical. How can I know it in practice? How can I put things behind me and press on without just burying the past? I suppose this is where counselling fits in. If God can bring glory to himself by all that I have been through, then I wish that he would get on with it! It all seems so purposeless. I know the theological answer to this irreverent request. I just need to know deep down. I need a good dose of patience as well as grace!

If there must be scars, then they must be the smallest that they can possibly be. I cannot carry anything unnecessarily from the past. Whatever that costs, we must get as far as we can. I still feel that there are buckets of tears to cry. On a good day I think of Peter and the children, and our lovely house, and I think 'Oh wow! We have got so much going for us'. Maybe I need less time thinking about the past and more time looking at the present and the future. I don't know where you go in counselling from here.

Next day.

Well here we are in the pits! I cannot ever tell you how

grateful I am that you phoned last night. You have no idea of what a lifeline those phone calls have been.

I guess Peter and I started to try and talk about the problems in the sexual side of our marriage. Last night! It has taken us this long to get almost over the pressure of life and home, and have the space to talk. We have been talking on and off all the time, but last night was the first major-length chat. Words cannot describe how sad and hard it was. It is now almost one o'clock the next day and I have not stopped crying. The hardest part was Peter's sadness, and almost grief, last night. So far I have just about hung on feeling that it is 'my' problem. When he said how hurt he felt I just heaped out and I haven't stopped. He said today that he didn't care if we never made love again in one sense. That condition he felt had to be agreed, so that I could feel free to deal with the abuse for myself and not so that we could make love easily as an end product. It helped me when he said that because I know that he is not just wanting me to sort it out so he will get more pleasure. He seems so upset by it all. It is good in a way that we are here, because we are having to hear each other, and we are both seeing it through. I am just so mad now. It was bad enough to think that he had damaged me, but now he has badly damaged Peter and hurt him. Why should he have stolen our pleasure? Why should he have touched me where Peter only had right to touch? Since he touched me, I feel ill and frightened if Peter does, how dare he steal that from us!

Last night we went through all the specific links where we both knew that being abused had affected my reactions. It was awful. I had enough ideas of my own, and Peter had even more! I feel sexually inept. Useless. How can I ever feel like a normal woman? I have no idea of what normal is. I am sick, sick, sick of it all. I cannot stop crying and hurting.

I have tried praying, but it is only between tears, and God feels as if he is 'out there somewhere'. There is supposed to be an upsurge of Bible-believing Christians in this area, but at the moment it feels like a completely God-forsaken place.

Next day.

I ache with sadness today for all I've lost, for all we have lost. Can God ever make up for all the years 'the locusts have eaten'? We really need some help and support if we are ever going to get through this.

I suppose that I am going to have to sign off and post this letter. I nearly phoned you this morning to ask you both to pray. Peter took all the children out again, so that I could have time on my own. It was a great idea, but I could have screamed with unhappiness by myself. He was pleased when I told him that I didn't ring you. We have just got to see this through together to a certain extent. I suppose it doesn't matter if you understand me through and through, Peter must, and that is what matters to me the most. That doesn't mean that we don't need help, it means the opposite. In some ways I have stopped trying to tell him how I feel because it hurts so much. Now we are really talking it is nearly killing us with the hurt, but I know it is a funny kind of progress.

I guess by the time you have received this we shall be in a different phase, but it has helped me just to write it. I have read it all to Peter and he says that it is not exaggerated!

Our love to you,
Peter and Rebecca

By the last week of the holiday we were completely exhausted. The feeling of grieving had not gone, and everything seemed to be such an effort. We both felt lonely and isolated. All we had was each other and three books. The children seemed to be oblivious of what was going on and still remember it as a beautiful holiday. I felt so disappointed in God. He did not seem to be meeting with me in my hurt and anger. Everything I had believed before suddenly seemed irrelevant and there was nothing to relieve the pain. The Lord did speak to me, however, in a most amazing way, and this gave me the only hope I could hold on to for the difficult months and years that lay ahead.

I had started to read the third book late one morning while the children were playing in the garden, as I wanted to read it before we went back home. I carried on reading it as we went along in the car that afternoon. We had planned to take the children to a beautiful cove where they could play on the beach. Once I had started to read, I felt compelled to read on. The story was about an American woman who had been abused as a child, and it charted how she received help. I was so moved by her account that I cried all the way through the book. I felt as if I had met the woman and we were hurting together.

The children could see that I was crying, whereas until then I had managed to keep my grief hidden. Peter took the children on to the sandy beach, and I tried to sit on the rocks at the edge and pray. I blurted out all my anger to God, the feelings of sadness and bitterness that constantly welled up inside me. I think I cried solidly for two hours. Peter would come over as often as he could and hug me, but I felt quite inconsolable, helpless, and empty. I practically shouted out to God just how angry I was, and as I did so, the arc of a rainbow came across the edge of the bay. I knew that the rainbow was a picture from God, reminding us that he was always with us, but I was still furious.

'What good is that?' I half prayed and shouted. 'I know you have promised to be with me, but what about the children? I need one arc for each of my four children. Let me know that you are with them, and care for them.' I felt then that I was a miserable failure as a mother. God, I believed, should have intervened and stopped the abuse. My children were now being affected – and why hadn't he stopped it? I was furious: I should have been able to enjoy the beauty of the scene before me with my family, but, because of the circumstances that was not possible. Nearly twenty-five years had elapsed, and I was still 'paying the price'.

I nearly fell off the rock in shock: as I expressed all this to

God, the rainbow came and went four times. It was such a special moment. I had called Peter over on the second arc and told him what was happening. Peter lovingly put his arms around me. 'See, God really does love us and care for us.'

I felt Peter was being infuriatingly simplistic, though, and I was still angry. It was probably just an amazing coincidence anyway, I thought. By now we were walking back to the car and ready to go home. I was still furious and wanted Peter to know that. 'Well, never mind the children. I need to know God loves *me*. Why doesn't he send a huge rainbow across the whole bay just for me?' I blurted out. Peter laughed, and we started to clip the children into their safety straps in the car. We had parked on top of a small hill, and Peter suddenly said, 'Look back, Rebecca. Quickly!'

There, stretching right across the bay, was the most beautiful rainbow that I had ever seen. I was stunned. My tears of sadness turned into tears of gratitude that I was loved by a God who certainly was not just 'out there somewhere', but who was right inside my situation. He longed to change the way I had been affected by things, and I knew I had to be more open to his ways. We took lots of photographs of the rainbow. I wanted to catch that moment for ever, as I felt God was so close to us. The rainbow stayed in the sky for a long time, and we were even able to drive further up the hills so that we could photograph it again.

Out of the holiday that had held so much pain, it became a very treasured and special memory for us both.

17

We returned from Scotland and John and Margaret carried on counselling me about the abuse. I had certainly stopped pretending to myself or them that there wasn't a problem. The three weeks of tears and pain had made me realise just how much I had been keeping hidden for so many years. Neither of them had ever counselled someone who had been abused before, so they did not know the main areas that would need to be dealt with, and much of the counselling was by trial and error.

I had counselling for the next four years, but I cannot describe to you a set of stages in clear progression, because it was not like that for me. Someone who has experience or training in helping those who have been abused would have appreciated some of the wider issues, and none of us were prepared for the length of time that counselling would be needed. I had envisaged that a couple of sessions would sort things out, but the further we delved into the damage, the more was unravelled. It was all very hard.

The first thing I had to do was to tell them exactly what had happened to me. This might sound obvious, but even though I had told Peter a bit about the abuse, I had never told the whole story in sequence. Nor had I spoken about the abuse while allowing my feelings to show – and I had simply related it as one would any normal childhood memory. For the first time I had to relate the pain of the experience and describe how the abuse had escalated. It was good not being hurried, and I was glad that someone wanted to listen to all the details, ones that I thought were important, but that adults at the time had not even thought about.

I was sure John and Margaret would not understand how

serious and awful it was for me. I wrongly believed that only if a person had intercourse with a child would it count as serious abuse. That had really troubled me, because it was about the only thing Mr Sutherland had not done, and I could not believe the amount of damage still caused without that act. I had not understood that the damage of abuse is not just related to the amount of physical harm, but also to the destruction of emotions. I had completely lost trust in myself and adults as a consequence of what had happened. He had robbed me of my very self in the ways he used me to gratify himself sexually.

When I first told the whole story to John and Margaret I hardly looked at them as I spoke. I was lost in the memory of it all. As I heard my voice speaking the words, I began to realise that I had made nothing up, and it had really happened to me. However much I had tried to distance myself from it all, it was still there. I could not run away from it. The mouth that spoke the words belonged to the same body that Mr Sutherland had abused. Becky could not stay 'frozen' for ever. When I had finished speaking, I looked up and saw tears in the eyes of both John and Margaret. They sat opposite me holding each other. Their actions spoke more than any words had done before.

John said that they were horrified at what had happened, and it was a terrible thing that Mr Sutherland had done to me. There was so much healing in their words. I felt such relief that I was not going mad and making everything up, for someone outside me was understanding the awful feelings inside my body.

For the next couple of sessions we went over every detail. I wanted to talk and talk about it, even though it hurt such a lot. As I talked I could remember everything so clearly, which was amazing, since I had hidden everything for so long. I was able to see as an adult what had happened to me as a child, whereas, previously I had never been able to feel it properly as either.

I found as I talked that I wanted to ask questions that I already knew the answers to. I felt that I needed someone else to tell me the answers. I suppose that the child Becky had never had a single question answered, and she was still asking them across the chasmic years of silence. I had always worried about what would have happened to Mr Sutherland in prison. As a child, I had wanted someone to explain to me what exactly he had done wrong to me. I needed to be told what a prostitute was. It might sound silly, but it was as if the child, when released to speak, needed to ask her questions, not those imposed by the counsellor. John and Margaret were very patient and understanding and explained everything in the same vein as I asked it. I was meeting the child in me for the first time and I needed to listen to her too.

Having got over the initial phase of coming out of denial, I then had to go painstakingly over all the areas where I had a distorted picture. There were four main areas of movement as I began to come to terms with all that the abuse had entailed. First, I had to move from a place of believing all the lies to finding out what the truth was about many areas in my life. I had such a distorted image of so many things that this was very tedious, but it was absolutely necessary. It was as if I had to reprogramme my mind. Second, I had to move from the place of utter grief about all that had happened to a place where I could live with the loss I had experienced. I could not stay crying and bewildered for ever – I had to get on with living. Third, I had to move from a place of raw anger, both at Mr Sutherland and at my parents for handling the situation as they did, to a place where I could direct my energies into useful ways of changing the situation for myself and others. Fourth, I had to leave the place of superficial forgiveness and go forward to a place of ongoing wholeness.

I cannot prescribe that everyone needs to move through these particular stages in the same way – I can only describe what happened for me. At the beginning of the counselling the direction we were going in was not at all clear. We were just vaguely drifting in the direction of healing. These four categories of movement have only emerged after the time of counselling, as I reflect on all the different areas we covered.

The counselling was almost spiral. We seemed to go over the same ground endlessly at times, but each time it was at a deeper level.

At first I could not handle much at all and could only move in very small stages. I had denied everything for so long that it was not easy to face the reality. Sometimes it was very frustrating: I wanted so much to declare that I was healed completely, that everything was fine. I was so proud that I could not bear to admit I still had areas of extreme weakness and vulnerability. I also could not bear to live with the pain of trying to come to terms with it all. It was so painful to remember and to look at some of the emotions, and it was such a struggle at times to change the way I was thinking and living. In some senses I had got used to living the way that I did, and to change was costly and difficult.

I have often thought about the blind man that Jesus healed. I wish the Bible gave us a record of what it was like for him on the first day after his healing. He had wanted all his life to see things clearly, he had prayed for it, and questioned why he couldn't see. Then one day he had an encounter with Jesus and was healed. Everyone, including himself, was thrilled and busy praising God. Yet I wonder how many times the poor man fell over because he had learned to walk without using his eyes. I wonder if he became frustrated because he was quicker and more efficient at doing things when his eyes did not work. I imagine that maybe, when he was tired and fed up, he would shut his eyes for a while just so that he could relax and get on with things the only way he knew how. Jesus did not just heal the man enough to see: he had to go on and *live* as a seeing man. That would have taken time and patience, not only on his part, but also for his friends. His healing would not have been complete if he had stayed on the roadside and been too scared to see how far he could venture now that he could see.

The same applied to me. There were many days when I had got so used to living with fear and panic attacks and avoiding the problems, that I got fed up with striving to be different. It seemed simpler to go back to the old way of feeling and looking at things. I needed friends to keep me 'with my eyes open', or the measure of healing I had received would have been lost. This meant that I had to keep striving towards healing and I could not afford to give up the effort. I found it particularly hard in counselling when I felt God was unusually close, and when a part of the experience seemed to be changed in some major way. I would feel so excited, so healed and whole. I was convinced that I would not need any more counselling, and that everything was now fine. On a couple of occasions I even suggested to John that I didn't need to see him any more. After a while, though, the underlying feelings of grief and depression would return and I knew there was more work to do. I guess that there are a lot of facets to healing someone who has been emotionally damaged to such an extent. I would not dispute that there may be people who have one major healing experience and never seem to suffer from any further after-effects. God is able to heal some people like that – and certainly wants everyone to be healed in some way. However, for whatever reason, we have to face the reality that God does not usually heal in this way when there is emotional damage.

When Joni Eareckson declares that she knows the healing power of God even though she is a quadriplegic in a wheelchair, people can believe it and understand it. Although initially some people did tell her that if she had more faith she could get out of her wheelchair, there is currently a correct and welcome acceptance of the fact that Joni is not physically healed, but she shows in her life a very beautiful example of the healing of the inner person. I have met her, and can testify to an inner beauty that makes the physical impairment almost irrelevant. In a similar way (and I know the analogy fails somewhat), people who have been abused, or have suffered other kinds of emotional damage, are in an invisible 'wheelchair', unable to 'get into' relationships, just as a wheelchair user might not be able to get into a building.

For myself, I know that my emotional development was thwarted in some areas at the age of nine. If this had been a physical stopping of development, people would have found it easier to be sympathetic and supportive. It is more difficult to live with the fact that part of you is emotionally frozen. Some parts may never be revitalised, although many will, through a lot of counselling and support. What is so difficult is learning to live with an impairment that no one can physically see, but that still restricts the person in the same way that buildings may for a wheelchair user. I am not suggesting that everyone who is emotionally damaged should throw their hands up in despair and say 'I am what I am and can never change'. However, there must be a degree of acceptance of the extent of the damage before change can take place.

It is so much easier to write this years later. I was always angry that I wasn't more healed, and felt that if I made more effort I could will myself to be whole. I have put so much energy into struggling to be healed. I have felt less Christian than anyone else, bordering on the edge of madness at times, because I have been unable to make up the difference. Now I see it is a process that can rarely be speeded up, and it hurts. I wish dearly that there was an instant solution. Sometimes I have been furious that God has not intervened and stopped the pain immediately, and that counselling has been the only way forward for me. Now I feel that God has always been alongside me and is moving me towards healing. Yes, there are times when I feel I am going backwards – and getting worse as well, if I am honest – but there are also occasions when I go forward a long way. God is there all the time and wants a healing that is deep and lasting, for all eternity.

18

The essence of abuse is lies. If the adult who abused faced the truth that he was damaging another person for his own selfish gratification, he would not abuse. If the child who was abused faced the truth that he or she had no alternative, was the victim of another person's crime, the damage would be much less.

Not only had my abuser lied in all that he was, said, and did, but my parents had also prevented me from finding out the real truth because, due to their denial, I was given wrong information. Unfortunately I based most of my life on the lies that had been ingrained in me. En route to healing, I have again had lies told to me. I do not believe, however, that my parents or those who sought to help have deliberately lied, and perhaps the word 'lie' may seem too strong a one to use. Through counselling and in my own thinking, I have had to make certain statements about what I have believed and what is the truth. There is a verse in the Bible that says, 'Then you will know the truth, and the truth will set you free' (John 8:32).

For anyone suffering from emotional damage, it may be helpful to analyse some of the lies on which they are basing their lives.

First, the child within me has screamed many lies – she believed for so long that it was all her fault. The way that I was treated when the abuse was discovered clearly gave the message to me that I had done something terrible, and the police and my mother certainly encouraged me to think that I had been responsible for everything that had happened. I even believed that an innocent man was going to prison because of my wickedness. I thought that I had sinned because I had allowed it to happen, even though I had no power to stop him and he used very subtle means to manipulate me. I was operating from a place of ignorance and simple trust. He acted from an adult perspective of understanding and power.

As a child, I wanted to protect Mr Sutherland. I yearned for everyone to like him, and to discover the lovely parts of his nature that I had got to know so well. I had hated the abuse, but had loved all the games before it. I had revelled in his attention, adoring the fun of visiting 'our special person'. I had enjoyed feeling grown up and singled out.

The lie I had believed was that all of this was wrong. These feelings were actually all valid and normal for a child. I had felt guilty about loving my abuser so much. From my childish point of view, I could not believe that the abuse mattered as much as it obviously did to other adults. As a child, it seemed like rather a minor aspect of a much bigger relationship.

Initially, I found it very hard as an adult to see what really did happen to me as a child. Now I absolutely hate all he did and was to me, but the child within me screams against that and loves him, without reservation. I have struggled to believe that he did not honestly delight in me for my own sake. If he had, he would never have abused me.

Mr Sutherland told me he did what he did for my good, because it made little girls happy. I believed that lie, and I had to come to terms with that in order to have a more satisfying sex life with my husband. When Peter seemed to want to give me pleasure, I could not believe that he was not just lying, and felt that I would suddenly discover what we were enjoying was wrong. My first experience of a sexual relationship had ended in disaster, and I had to relearn appropriate responses when I was married.

As a child I had taken on responsibility for Mr Sutherland's well-being, and even as an adult I found myself trying to defend him in counselling sessions. I could not bear to think of his sin. I hated to think that this gentle and lovely man was so wicked. The child had to grow up and face the awful truth: my abuser did not love me at all. He showed me no real love. He wanted his own delights, his own satisfaction. I was an object, that was the real abuse.

I felt so guilty that I had taken the money he gave us, and I felt there was truth in the judge's statement that I was a prostitute. I had indeed allowed him to do what he wanted for money, so what was the difference?

It took a lot of counselling to come to the place where I realised that I was a normal child, whereas Mr Sutherland was a paedophile of some cunning, who had quickly discovered how to manipulate me emotionally so that he could satisfy himself sexually. I had to reach the point of surrendering him to God and saying that he was no longer my burden. I had done so much to try and make things right for the 'sin' I felt I had committed – now I had to accept that I had not sinned, but that he had.

The process seemed endless. The rational part of me knew it wasn't my fault, but the emotional part still felt entirely responsible. I had to accept he was totally responsible for his own actions and to stop inwardly trying to make things right. I could scarcely bear to believe that he hadn't honestly loved me at all. I felt he was the first person to really enjoy me as I was, and to recognise that I had been wrong in this judgement was a terribly hard thing to do.

My father had given me the unspoken message that I was only really wanted if I could be perfect. I felt he was disappointed in the child I was: as far as he was concerned, I was too shy, too silly, too emotional. He didn't seem to want to spend time with me, or to listen to how I was feeling. I desperately craved the attention that Mr Sutherland had given me. How hard as an adult to come to terms with the fact that my own father had given me wrong information about my own worth. I was of infinite value in the eyes of God just as I was, but the first two men who had an influence in my life told me otherwise.

Another lie that I believed was that other people only wanted me in the same way that Mr Sutherland had wanted me: so that I could serve them. Slavishly, I had lived to please everyone else as much as I could. I craved for people to need me. I didn't feel that there was anything within me that was worthwhile, so I had to resort to doing things for other people all the time. I wrongly believed that only if people were using me could I satisfy them. I found it almost impossible to say no to any demands, however unreasonable. In fact, the more outrageous the demands, the more satisfied I felt.

One of the difficulties was that this kind of behaviour is encouraged so often by Christians. People rarely consider that the workaholics in the Church may have some kind of emotional difficulty, which means they are never satisfied with themselves. Rather, they are seen as sacrificially serving Christ. If you listen to some Christians talking about their day, you will spot what I mean. People ask for prayer for something, but only after having listed all the other things they must do, to make sure that everyone knows they are busy. We have all done it to some extent, but we have to be careful that we don't make something sound virtuous which for some may honestly be sin.

I once heard someone say that God would not love me any more or less if I lay down on the floor for one year and did nothing, rather than rushing round trying to do things for him. What a mind-blowing thought! I had believed the lie that I have to serve God as a mindless slave, and that he will be satisfied with nothing less. Mr Sutherland only wanted me for what I could do for him. God, however, certainly does not delight in us just for our actions, but for being the people he created us to be in the first place.

I also had to face the truth that other people could cope with my limitations and weaknesses better than I could myself. I always felt that people merely tolerated me – I could not believe that they might love me despite all the things wrong about me. I wanted perfection, and it took me a long time to realise that others could cope with less. On the occasions when I was depressed, I tried to compensate for it and hide my negative feelings by doing more. The fact that this nearly destroyed me physically and emotionally didn't seem to matter to me. I hated the thought that if any of my friends realised how awful I felt inwardly, then they would leave me. I wanted to be there for them: I was quite happy when they found things a struggle, or if they were going through bad times. Then I could patiently come alongside them and it didn't matter at all. It was hard to learn the lesson that they could, and would, do the same for me.

Another lie I believed was that I had to be doomed to a life of trusting no one. As I have said, I lost trust in myself and in others, especially men, as a result of the abuse. I had to learn that even though one man had let me down so horrendously, it was wrong to assume that all men would do the same. Sometimes a person would let me down in the normal course of events and often I would become very angry and overreact. It has been a gradual process of learning that it is wrong to make everyone else pay the price of Mr Sutherland's abuse.

Having faced the fact that Mr Sutherland was a liar, I tried quite hard to find a justification for his lies. I read somewhere that people who have been abused themselves are more likely to abuse. I have lately discovered that this is quite unhelpful, and statistically not very reliable. When I learned first of that idea, though, I clung to it like a lifeline as a justification for Mr Sutherland's actions. I reasoned that it had probably happened to him, so he could not be held responsible for what he did to me. It is hard now to accept that this is rubbish. It doesn't matter what one has experienced: it does not justify them doing the same thing to someone else. It might be more understandable, but it is no less wrong.

I have had to face some hard truths about my parents. They were both well-known leaders in the church, and everyone looked up to them as models of a happy marriage and good parenting. It was difficult to accept that even though they were happily married and were doing their best at bringing up their children, they made some serious mistakes. Furthermore, their mistakes had major consequences in my life. When other Christians told me just how helpful my parents had been in seeing them through the various crises in their own lives, and how they had been such a shining example, it was difficult to accept that any error on their part was not caused by me. In the first instance, my mother handled the discovery of the abuse appallingly. She just shut it out, having previously offloaded all the guilt on to the innocent party – me. She sought help neither for herself nor for me. It was a dreadful mistake that she did not tell my father. By making that decision, she effectively cut off a huge area of my life, so that I have been unable to develop my relationship with my parents as fully as I should have been able to. They, unknowingly, have been unable to share with each other and grow through the trauma. Instead, it has acted as a silent buffer.

The burden of the secret that has been mine for so many years has been immense and very damaging. Two years ago my younger sister decided to talk to my mother about what had happened. Lizzie showed her little mercy, and even went as far as to say that it wasn't the abuse that had caused so much damage but my mother's reaction to it. My mother was horrified at this sudden revelation, and claimed that she had never realised just how serious it all was. She thought it had been a minor incident and had no idea of the time-scale or the extent of the damage done to us. My mother then talked to me about it, still denying that she had understood the implications. She also said that since my father was so busy with his work and the church, she had found herself bringing us up almost as a single parent and had felt that she was better off handling the situation herself.

I had never thought of how it had been for her, and I did find it helpful to understand how she saw it. Having said that, she was still wrong in what she did. More recently, I have asked her to tell my father about it at long last. I am so sick of there being any secrets at all in my life. It is getting more and more difficult to explain the conferences and retreats I have gone on to help me come to terms with the abuse, and I sometimes have to be quite deceitful to my parents. I feel this is hurtful and unnecessary. I know that I did nothing wrong and I do not have to hide what happened – except of course, to my father.

Sadly, my mother is still refusing to tell him. She maintains that he would not cope with it; moreover, it would mean admitting that the adage we were brought up on – 'There are no secrets in our marriage' – is a lie. I also feel my father should take his share of responsibility for what went wrong. Although all his efforts to work hard were sincere, they were also seriously misguided. I cannot imagine my own husband not noticing one of our children being unhappy or not their normal selves. Yet my father managed to miss two of his three children suffering at least eighteen months of abuse and the pain of subsequent discovery. It is a testimony to the amount of time he was otherwise occupied that he managed not to notice anything at all. I have had to acknowledge that even though I love my parents dearly, they have made some dreadful mistakes, and that these aren't just in the past – they still continue to make the same ones!

Christians have also given me some wrong information in their attempts to be helpful. Again, I do not mean this in a judgmental sense, but rather as a statement of fact. I believe all this wrong information has been given in the most well-intentioned way, but until I disentangle some of the lies I cannot be reconciled to the truth. One such lie is that people who sincerely believe and have enough faith are always healed completely. The reality is that they are not. I am speaking as someone who sincerely believes. I have asked God for faith, since it is his gift anyway. I believe God could heal me instantly, but the truth is that he has not.

Another lie I have been faced with is the misuse of the verse, 'In all things God works for the good of those who love him, who have been called according to his purpose'. (Rom. 8:28). Now I do believe this is true, and ultimately I have faith that everything I have experienced will be worked into a bigger picture of eternal good.

What I have also found to be the truth is that our petty attempts to discover what good has come out of something is not a justification for what has happened. Let me explain. If one of my children died, I could imagine that good might come out of that terrible experience. People might come to a saving knowledge of Jesus at the funeral, for example or other

parents might find new love for their wayward child when
they saw that we had lost ours. Even though these things
might help in our loss, they would never be enough to stop
the pain of our grief. They might or might not be helpful, but
they would not be a good enough reason for accepting that
the death of our child was right. In some mysterious way
I believe God does use everything, but quite often other
Christians' attempts to salve pain by pointing to this verse
adds to the grief experienced.

People have tried telling me that I am more helpful and
sensitive as a listener because I have experienced intense
personal pain. People have pointed to the work in the
community that I do as a marvellous way in which God has
used my past experiences. Now both of these things might
be true, but they do not justify what happened to me. It would
still have been better if the abuse had never happened. It was
still a terrible sin that Mr Sutherland committed.

In the world that God initially created there was no abuse
and there was no death. Sometimes I feel that as Christians
we feel almost embarrassed at what God has allowed to
happen. He does not, however, need us to clutch at good
things that have come out of bad to verify that he is good
and has our best interests at heart. It is a natural desire
in us to look at the good coming out of terrible evil, and
maybe it is something we can do for ourselves, but I think it
is rarely helpful to share this with the person who is suffering
at the time.

I also wrongly believed the lie told me by my mother, that
if anyone found out what had happened to me there would be
terrible consequences. This lie meant that I had tried to hide
anything to do with the abuse from all my friends, and was so
ashamed of my need for counselling that I told hardly anyone
about that either. The initial attempt at telling someone what
had happened was my first go at seeing if it was a truth or a
lie that I had been told. When I first told my closest friends
about the abuse, I told them almost dispassionately; as if it
was just a piece of interesting information. I described it all
as an unfortunate episode in my life that had been completely

dealt with. I was not being deliberately deceitful: it was the only way I could handle telling anyone.

After more counselling I was able to go further with close friends and say I was having to deal with the after-effects, but I was still coping well. As time went on, I had to admit, not only to close friends but to a wider circle, that I was desperately struggling with the consequences of abuse and I was barely all right at all. Every time I told someone else what had happened I dreaded that they would want nothing more to do with me, that they would think I was dirty and what I had done was shameful. No one ever reacted like that, however. Everyone I told confirmed the truth, that it was not my fault and something damaging had happened to me.

For many friends it was a relief to find out why I acted so strangely at times! I had not done such a brilliant job at covering up as I had thought, and people had realised that something was seriously wrong, but had never been able to identify it. There are lots of examples of this. I had unwittingly developed a pattern of always wanting my children home with me after school. Often I would go along to the school with other mothers, who might suggest some of the children went to play at their house. I had never understood why, but the very suggestion made me frightened, and I would make excuses as to why they had to be home with me. I thought it was because I was a caring mother, but it was not based on rationality – it was, rather, a deep fear that they would be damaged on their way home from school. When I told one mother about the abuse, she mentioned the numerous occasions when I had refused her hospitality, although I had often offered to have her children at my house. As soon as I realised the cause of my fear I was able to change my behaviour and she was able to help me. It has obviously been much better for the children too.

Another person who had been abused confided in me that she was terrified if anyone else offered to take her child to playgroup, even though it would often have been very helpful. She was afraid they would abuse her children as soon as she was out of sight. If people don't know the reasons behind such seemingly odd behaviour, they can make the mistake of seeing abused people as being antisocial.

I found friends desperate to help, and very understanding once they had some information. It was so much easier when I told more people, because I no longer had to carry the burden of the secret alone, and they were more able to help me at times of deep despair and pain. Ironically, I was also able to help them more, too, because our friendships were based on far more openness. Once one of my main masks was down, some of theirs could safely be taken down too.

There were times when I had to say that the counselling was desperately hard and I felt as if I was falling to pieces completely. My friends could then come alongside me and say in their actions and their love, 'We are brothers and sisters together, we'll pick up the pieces together. You are you, and that is OK.' Prior to admitting the effects of the abuse, I was desperately trying to keep my 'Mrs Got-it-together' image in place. Now I have a more 'Mrs Roller-coaster' image. I preferred the first picture, but the second is more real, and is a lot easier to live with for all concerned! The truth is that God loves me just as I am, and he is not disappointed.

19

I was very surprised at my response when I first read about the damage caused by abuse. The only time I have felt as bereft was when someone very close to me died. Grief and bereavement were a part of coming to terms with what had happened, but it was all made harder as I did not recognise my feelings as being those of someone grieving: I honestly believed that I was weak minded.

I could not speak about the abuse without crying – I could not even say the words at first. Eventually I learned to talk about my experiences without weeping, but only if I resorted to an objective description of what had happened. As soon as I remembered any feelings associated with it, the tears came.

At the outset it was is if the child in me had completely died, for I had lived so long without listening to her. Not only did she have a separate name, 'Becky', but she had experienced so much that I did not want to remember. At first, I could not even say 'I', but always talked about the abuse as something that happened in the third person, as if Becky was someone else. I would say, 'She did not like what he did to her, but she didn't know how to say no.' I found the only way that I could relate to 'Becky' was to think about the *good* times I had in the woodshed, but I could not bear to think about what else had happened.

After someone close to you has died, sometimes you find yourself looking for them. You imagine that they cannot possibly be dead: they will come round the corner any minute. You search for them, not believing they have gone. The same was true of my experience with abuse. I was desperately searching for the child within myself; sometimes

I almost caught a glimpse of her, but I could not relate to her in any way. I did not want to admit that she was even a part of me. Although the adult could accept that she had done no wrong, the child felt so guilty and horrible that I did not want to associate with her.

I grieved so much for the child who was lost in the woodshed, for the innocent child who had skipped round the park the wrong way. Nothing was the same for me after that experience. I had entered the woodshed happy and trusting – I was a normal child with simple ideas about life, and wanted to serve God with all I had. Mr Sutherland had turned me into a child who hated her motives, had lost her ability to trust, and despised her own body and her very self. I didn't feel I could ever get back to her.

I mourned for the adult that I might have been if I had not been so damaged. I know it is impossible to know exactly what I would have been like, but I grieved for the years I had lost trying to bury the memories, for the years of pain I had experienced because I was hurting so much. I was sad for that part of the relationship with my parents that had been irretrievably lost. I cried for the marriage that, although wonderful in spite of everything, had still suffered dreadfully. I wept for the time I had been unable to enjoy my children to the extent that I might have done if I had not been trying to learn to live with the damage of abuse. I mourned for the relationship that I had not been able to have with a God I loved, because my image of him had been so distorted by Mr Sutherland. There was just so much to be sad about, such a lot had been damaged or destroyed. I know that a great deal of the loss was retrievable through much help and support, but it was not possible to avoid the grieving. I found I had to grieve deeply all that had gone, in order to get to the place where I could find a hope for healing.

At first all I could do was to weep continuously. Sometimes people would ask what I was crying about, and in a strange way that seemed an irrelevant question. I hardly knew myself what was so sad; I only knew that there was no other appropriate response at that stage except to weep.

For so many years I had been unable to use words to describe the pain I was in – tears had become the only way I could communicate. The most helpful response was when people let me cry, when they did not demand that I stopped, and were not embarrassed by me. I nearly always felt terribly awkward and ashamed that my grief was so open and public. It would have been more socially acceptable to cry so much if somebody had died, but as it was, I could never explain what the matter was. Very often I did not know what had triggered me into such sadness at that moment, but the tears were always there, just under the surface. Sometimes in church I would just weep and weep, and people must have wondered what on earth was wrong.

I also experienced the grief in a sense of total emptiness and a feeling of being lost. At this stage it was almost impossible to cry. There was a restlessness in me that searched for an end to the pain but could find nothing. Nothing seemed to matter, nothing seemed relevant – I just had to go through the motions of everything, and could feel nothing. It was as if I had run out of tears and was trying to search for a place where everything would be all right again, even though I knew intellectually that it couldn't.

Sometimes the depression that had been so marked in my earlier life became quite serious again. A sort of black darkness seemed to engulf me and I felt unable to stop it. At these times it did not matter what ground had been gained in counselling: everything seemed to go. I would be back being the child who hated herself, who hated everyone except her abuser. At these times, it would seem as though God had left me altogether, and nothing made any sense at all. The only grip I had on reality was to keep going through the motions with the children and keep life outwardly normal, although inside I was struggling to keep going and could hardly make emotional ends meet.

The only way out of this depression was to keep busy. This dulled the pain in the short term, but had the longer-term effect of making it all harder to come to terms with, because I kept pushing it away from me.

I would try to emerge from these stages of grief by searching for anything that might help to alleviate the pain. I read as many books as I possibly could on the subject of abuse. I was trying to discover if someone else held the key to not feeling such acute pain for so long. Although each of them helped in some way, none of them had an 'answer'. I listened to items on the radio and watched television programmes on abuse in order to try and understand more about what had happened to me. This often made things worse as I realised how terribly others had suffered, and their loss did not make mine any easier to bear.

I wrote extensively as a way of expressing all my feelings. I hoped that by getting everything on to paper I would be able to understand it all to a greater extent. This did help, and when I saw what I had written I could begin to achieve some relief as I had been able to express the pain in something more tangible than tears. Without meaning anyone else to read them, I wrote letters to my abuser, to my parents, even to 'Becky', and learned a lot from each of them.

I now want to be involved with setting up a group for survivors of sexual abuse so that we can work through our pain together. I could not even have considered such an idea in the earlier stages, but now I feel it would be a useful thing to do. I would not just be doing it to help others, but because I have discovered that one way forward for myself is to talk about what has happened and what is happening now. I have needed to talk endlessly about the whole subject. I had been unable to speak about it for so long, that now, each time I talk about, it is as if I am a little more healed. I can break the silence now and I will not be quiet again. Every time I speak I am affirming that the abuse wasn't my fault. I am speaking out all the things that are the truth about my situation, and this has helped me to deny the power of the lies.

I have been blessed with friends who have understood my need to talk. Never have they told me that I should be over it by now, and they have never told me I should stop. Yes, I have needed counselling, but the ability of my friends just to be ordinary and listen has helped me so enormously. I have been with friends who have lost a child, and I know that years later they still need to talk about that child, the day their child died, the feelings they have now, the memories they still cherish, and the memories that they find hard to bear. It is similar with abuse: I need to talk about it, for words and tears are my only way of showing the pain, and they are my way forward. The ability of my friends to speak wisely has never seemed as important as their gift of being with me, listening to me, and loving me, just the way I am.

20

When Peter and I first began to realise the extent of the damage caused by Mr Sutherland's sexual greed, we both became extremely angry. It is almost impossible to describe in words the extent of the rage we both felt. At times this feeling was so overwhelming that it seemed to assume an identity of its own, and swept over me as though I could not control it. I was angry that I was still paying the price for what he had done so many years before. I was angry that Peter and the children had been involved, that the extent of the abuse had spread past me. I realised that my friends had also been affected, because my emotions had been so damaged. The ramifications of what he had done were so extensive. Rationalising and trying to find an explanation for why he had done it seemed a complete waste of time when anger was present. I just wanted to scream and kick and fight with everything in me to express that rage. I didn't know what to do with it. I had never experienced such a strong emotion. The panic attacks, which had seemed to come from nowhere, began to be understandable for the first time.

I only went into a state of panic when the anger and anxiety I was experiencing could no longer be confined within words or tears. It was then that I went wild. This explains why only a man could trigger me into a panic attack; if a man was trying to 'come near to me' in an emotional way, or if I thought he might move towards me physically, the panic and anger rose in me and I responded. The urge to fight and hit and destroy was one of the most frightening features of the panic attack, and yet it was the only way I could express the rage inside me. The more I tried to bottle that up, the more I physically shook. If someone used the name 'Becky' instead of 'Rebecca', I started to panic. The name 'Becky' unlocked the part of me that was hurting so much, and since I could not verbalise how that part of me was feeling at that stage, I just resorted to panic.

I found it so hard that I could feel so violent and aggressive. Normally I am not a physically destructive person at all – I can hardly bear to swat a fly – and the thought that I would want to attack someone when that panic feeling swept over me was terrible. Now, as I look back, I realise that the panic attacks were not random events: they were expressions, albeit inadequate ones, of the feelings I had hidden for so long. I still get the first feelings of panic when I am in situations that I feel are threatening, but now I have learned to listen to why they are threatening and deal with them in more appropriate ways, much to the relief of those trying to help me!

Sometimes I am aggressive in a verbal way. When something seems wrong or threatening to me, then I can be very angry in the way that I address someone. I have tried to curb this, as it has landed me in all kinds of trouble! One of the deacons in the church was trying to organise the creche rota and suggested that mothers should be the only ones on the list. Instead of being able to argue my case in a rational and reasoned manner, I issued this great tirade about how wrong it all was, and made Churchill's wartime speeches sound like an invitation to a picnic. I now realise that, although it was reasonable to disagree with him, my response was disproportionate to the issue in hand. On reflection, I see that I felt he, as a man, was trying to control me as a woman and decide what I should do. That, for an abused person, is like a red rag to a bull. Incidentally, the effect of my speech was quite stunning, and the deacon himself signed up for the rota!

It is not wrong to be angry. I feel it is a necessary and essential part of the grieving process after abuse. To be honest, though, it is a ghastly thing to experience in its extreme form. I did not find that I experienced anger in one stage and then it was all gone. At first there was a huge amount, but even after lots of counselling there are still times when something happens and the anger rises up in me all over again. It is like the grieving process. When someone dies, you may feel you are just starting to come to terms with it, then suddenly a little thing happens and you find yourself weeping once again. It feels as if nothing has changed and that the grief is just as acute as when the person first died. That is how it is for me. I know that I have had so much support, and realise I have had a great deal of counselling, but there are times when the grief and the anger almost overwhelm me again. When that happens I feel that all the counselling and all the pain have been a waste of time, but in reality these times are shorter now and I am able to find ways through.

I have found it helpful to direct into useful channels the anger that could otherwise destroy me and those around me. I have only been able to do this after a lot of counselling, and I don't think that it is healthy to do it too soon. Otherwise, you are in danger of hiding the anger rather than using it as a tool. In one sense I have good cause to be angry: I was violated and I should not have been. I feel that I have to choose how I am going to react to that. I can either choose to hug that anger to myself and, in a way, revel in it, or I can start to take action that would help others to express their own pain, and possibly help prevent the same thing happening to anyone else. When the rage is directed inwards, however, I find I hate myself. The anger seems to be the veil through which I observe myself, and I despise what I see. I feel worthless, useless, and no good to anyone. This inward anger quickly leads to depression, the feelings of grief become paramount, and I am on a downward spiral.

Yet it can be destructive to channel my energy into work. Workaholism is an almost universal complaint of those who have been abused. This can be good, and at least it is a more constructive channel for the grief and the anger, but it can work in a negative way. Sometimes I have driven myself beyond all reasonable limits physically and emotionally because I feel unable to stop. I am scared that if I stop, the powerful feelings associated with the abuse will overwhelm me. The silly part is that, the more I overdo things, the more likely that is to happen anyway, so I find myself in a 'Catch 22' situation! Fortunately, Peter and some of my friends can point out to me that I am doing this and they help me to see how I can put a stop to it. It is not easy for them because sometimes it doesn't matter what they say – I am convinced that everything I am doing is essential and that I could not possibly give any of it up. Indeed, in isolation everything I do is justifiable, but it is sometimes impossible for any human to do it all together. When I have been doing too much for too long, I reach an overload. It is then that I just cry a lot and am quite hopeless for a while. During this time I am unable to do anything for anyone. I can hardly answer the phone or the door, and I don't want any personal contact. This type of roller-coaster lifestyle is not ideal, but at the moment it is the only one I can work!

On one occasion a counsellor was trying to point out to me that I could not possibly satisfy everyone. I was not impressed with this, so I remonstrated that Jesus had told the story about the Good Samaritan and that we were supposed to help people and not walk past them. 'Yes,' said the counsellor, 'but he only picked up the first man he came across. If there had been an injured man every hundred yards down the road, he would not have been able to meet each of their needs.' I didn't like to admit it then, but he did have a point!

One of the most creative ways in which I have been able to direct my anger and energy is into a clothing store. I know that seems an unlikely way to come to terms with sexual abuse, but for me it has been an important lifeline. As I mentioned earlier, we started to get clothes arriving at our house for recycling, initially from the mothers in the daytime study club. Word started to spread, and eventually we had loads and loads of clothes arriving at the house. Now this seemed a practical and useful way to be a workaholic! By using my organisational skills (anger, when directed properly, is a brilliant driving force!), I could match demand with supply.

I discovered that since we were in recession there was a lot of poverty within the church. A high proportion of people there were trying to manage on state benefits that were unrealistically low. The mortgage rate had hit an all-time high, and there were some couples whose mortgage exceeded their wages at the worse stages. How on earth could these people find clothes for themselves and their children?

The number of people using the store increased all the time, and more people became involved in helping me sort out the clothes. One Sunday a lady came to our church and we invited her and her young son to lunch. We discovered that she was living in a local women's refuge, which we had not even realised existed until then. Women who are in any kind of danger are able to run to such places for safety. Some of the women eventually return to their partners, but many of them do not. If they run to escape immediate violence, they often arrive at the refuge with nothing except what they are wearing.

We discovered that this was the case for the woman who had come to lunch. We took her into the garage and went through the sacks of clothes. She was thrilled. I had thought we already experienced poverty in the church until I was faced with a woman who had practically nothing. She was so excited that she asked if she could bring the other women from the refuge to our house, so that they could all have clothes.

I felt ashamed when I saw them. I felt guilty at the wardrobe of clothes I had, and knew that I had to do something more to help. I felt such an empathy with these women. I knew that they had been abused by their partners, if not sexually, then certainly physically or emotionally. It mattered to them that they had clothes to wear that made them feel special. The majority of women who came through the refuge had lost their self-respect because of what had been done to them, and I could identify with that. I could not help them through counselling because I was still too mixed up emotionally myself even to contemplate such a thing, but this was something practical I could do.

When the clothes started to come in at a rate that was beyond reason, I approached the leadership of the church and asked them if we could use a large storeroom that was only full of things that no one claimed or wanted, but had been left there over the years. They agreed, thinking there would just be a few bags to add to the others. The problem was that the more space we had, the more people we were able to serve, and the increased publicity meant that still more people gave us clothes! We had to get rid of all the rubbish in the room, and use every inch of available space. Within a year, we were handling over sixty sacks a fortnight. Word quickly spread round the community, and soon we were opening the store for people referred to us by Social Services, the Probation Service, and Community Health Workers.

The whole thing was tremendously hard work, but it gave me so much satisfaction and fun. Our relationship with the workers at the refuge had developed to the extent that they would ring us up each time someone had arrived who needed clothes, and we would open up the store for them. I found the experience of being with these women at such a point of crisis very moving. When the women were looking for clothes, all of them searched for clothing for their children before they looked for themselves. Sometimes women would be about to leave and I would point out that they had taken nothing for themselves at all. Sometimes the physical marks on the women were obvious, often they were dazed and in a state of shock. It might not seem much to offer them clothes, but without them they could not send their children to school or have any hope of beginning a new life.

The work in the clothing store continued to develop, and eventually we were able to convert that area of the church to a proper clothing shop, the only difference being that nothing cost anything! We were able to send clothes that were surplus to our requirements to other outlets, and discovered through this simple work a very effective way of serving the community.

Was the system ever abused? Of course it was! One lady came and took sackloads of clothes, time after time. This was quite acceptable until I realised that her seven children were never dressed in anything but the latest fashions from the high street shops. On further investigation we discovered that she was selling everything she was getting! Another woman came and kept on taking loads of clothes for her children. The amount she took was excessive, but I did not like to doubt her integrity. However, after three weeks she left the refuge and we had a call to say that when the workers had gone into her room they had discovered it full of clothes from the church. The problem was that all of them were dirty: she had basically had a three-week holiday at my expense. Instead of doing any washing she had come to the church for more clothes! We had to wash the whole lot and get everything back to the store. I had thought that Mr Sutherland had taken away my ability to trust, but I realised in this episode that I had trusted the woman against all reason – the little girl in me had obviously not been destroyed!

As a child, I had so desperately wanted to tell Mr Sutherland about Jesus, but now (misguidedly) felt that I could never risk that again because of the consequences it had in my life. In the clothing store, however, I have found a means of showing the love of Jesus in a practical way, and have found I can silently pray for everyone as they use the store. To the onlooker, the clothing store is nothing more than a useful exercise in recycling. To me, it has become a channel of healing and wholeness and a way of directing my anger in a positive and constructive way.

As I have struggled to come to terms with the abuse I have increasingly come into contact with others who have been abused. Part of me hates meeting anyone who has been abused, since I feel that I can hardly handle my own pain, let alone share the pain of others. However, I also find a healing in meeting others, and I am forced to realise that I am not the only person this has happened to. Many people have suffered far worse abuse, and many have had much greater damage done to them. I feel I am just the tip of a large and terrible iceberg which we must do something about.

I have been in contact with a Christian Survivors Group and have found it has helped me not to feel so isolated. Whilst everyone has different experiences, there are some very strong common strands that are helpful to understand. I have learned that my own experiences do not mean that I can offer any solutions in this book that will sort out the problem for others. The most I can do is to say what happened to me and trust it will be helpful.

The survivors group, and the activities they have organised, have made me want to go back to my church and call them to action. I had previously thought that I was only concerned about abuse because it had happened to me, but I have now met many people who have not been abused but have listened to the pain of others and know they have to act. The statistics are frightening.

I know change will not happen overnight, but I must do anything I can to help those who have been abused move towards healing, and anything I can to prevent the abuse happening. I have become involved with the local school programme for sex education and now they are looking at the Kidscape programme (see p.200). I have been invited to speak to a group of ministers about abuse and the Church, and to speak to other groups of leaders in the area where I live. I am now working towards setting up our own local survivors group, because there are so few in the country and they are quite inaccessible to many.

I have started a community night at the church so that families can spend the evening together, single parents can have friendship and their children can experience a wider family. This might seem a small thing, but it is working towards building up a healthy family picture. It is wrong to keep promoting the closed family where abuse can go unnoticed for years. We have to come out from structures which pass as 'good and Christian', but which make children obey their parents to the point of allowing them to abuse them and then isolate them from others, so that they cannot tell anyone what is happening behind the closed walls.

We all need to do anything we can to help build good relationships right across the church and the community round it. It has been good for us as a family that all we are doing within the church involves our children. They help with sacks of clothes and the store, and they come to the community nights. We are doing all we can to redress the balance of my upbringing; our own children are part of what God has called us to do.

I find it particularly difficult in any area where I feel that women are being made vulnerable and used to satisfy men in whatever way, not just sexually. For me this is an aspect of life that has to be fought and we should try and change, even in small ways. I appreciate that men have also been abused, and that women are abusers too. I have to guard against sounding like a militant feminist or man hater! I am neither. However, it is wrong if anyone tries to overpower another person to satisfy him- or herself, and to this extent we are all guilty of abusing others. As Christians we should set an example which really shows that in Christ there are no unequal relationships. There is a verse in Galatians which is the goal we should be moving towards to eradicate abuse of any kind: 'There is neither Jew nor Greek, slave nor free, male nor female, for you are all one in Christ Jesus,' (Gal. 3:28). This does not allow for any power struggle. There is no space here for manipulation or self-gratification – we are all one and do not have any personal rights over each other.

I have moved a long way from an anger that consumes and controls me to an anger that is moving and being used constructively. It has become for me a useful driving force, although I still have to guard against the excesses. We do not, however, have a God who is never angry. One only has to read the Psalms to appreciate that God is angry at injustice, abuse, pain and suffering, and he reaches out to help. I have previously been ashamed of my anger because it has been so destructive, but I am gradually learning that it does not have to be that way.

21

I have found that my understanding of forgiveness has changed considerably since the first time I went to see Mr Sutherland. In one sense, I don't regret going in the way that I did and I believe God told me to do it. I think it was right to go and see him and say I had forgiven him in the best way I knew how at the time. In retrospect, however, I see that I used that incident to close me off from further healing for many more years. I had believed that forgiveness was the ultimate thing that I had to do, and there was nothing further. What I did not appreciate then was that I needed to start off on the road towards forgiving him for my own sake rather than his, and that my forgiving was an ultimate goal, not the end of the incident.

Some people have thought that the act of forgiveness itself is wrong, and that there is an implication of the innocent assuming some guilt. I believe that this is a complete misunderstanding of the nature of forgiveness. When you forgive someone you are not in any way saying that what they have done wrong to you is unimportant. In fact, if it was unimportant there would be no need for forgiveness – you would just carry on and ignore the situation. Real forgiveness, however, can only take place when you have some understanding of the sin and the damage involved.

When we went to forgive Mr Sutherland we hardly understood what we were doing. It was more a gesture of goodwill than a heartfelt statement of forgiveness for what he had done and the damage he had caused. Subsequently, I found it so hard every time I had negative or hateful thoughts about Mr Sutherland. After all, I reasoned, I had forgiven him, therefore I couldn't feel like this any more, so there must be something wrong with me.

Now I see forgiveness much more as a process than a one-off act. Forgiveness is saying to someone that what they did *was* terrible. He damaged me so extensively I have not fully faced it all yet. I have, however, made the decision that I am not going to hold on to him or his memory. I will separate from myself both him and the sin he committed against me. There has to be some kind of setting aside of the experience, but I do not want anyone to confuse this with forgetting it. I never will do that, but I will move away from the pain, leaving the sin where it belongs: with the abuser.

Forgiveness, which is understood as a letting go of someone else's sin, frees the person who is sinned against to go on living more fully. Forgiveness helps the person who is wronged far more than the person who did the wrong. Very rarely can restitution be made after abuse, although this is not completely impossible. The abuser must accept full responsibility for the sin and have a thorough understanding of the extent of the damage caused. He or she must be prepared to seek any means of change, so that past actions will not be repeated, and to make restitution as fully as is humanly possible, otherwise there is no basis for forgiveness, except at a very superficial level. For myself, I found that I could move along the road to forgiveness far more easily when I realised that Mr Sutherland was never my problem. God had seen everything he had done to us secretly and God could judge him. In other words, I released my right for his apology or restitution on to a God who would demand an account of his actions. I had wanted it right between Mr Sutherland and me, but I had, somehow, to let him go. This was a much more meaningful place of forgiveness, rather than simply saying that I forgave him.

Within the Church there may be a quick response to the abused person that says: you must learn to forgive the abuser – you will never be healed until you do. But there is no help to be found in just saying the words, and unless it is at the end of a long process of help and support, the abused cannot even understand the meaning of forgiveness because they have not appreciated the extent of the damage. The abused or the abuser often has little idea of the damage that has been caused. There have been times when I think abused people are expected to forgive in order that those around them should feel better! It is as if all we want is a neat set of answers and everything nicely sewn up. It goes something like this: 'You were hurt. Jesus says forgive those who do you wrong. Forgive the person who hurt you. Your hurt is no longer a problem. Let's get on with the next person.' I know this is a gross over-simplification, of course, but it is wrong to impose on people something that in reality could take them a lifetime.

Forgiveness, even if you arrive at it, will not wipe out the scars. There will still be damage. I don't think you can actually speed up the process either, which makes it difficult. Although I cannot speak for anyone else, in my experience I have found that complete forgiveness is not a place I ever reach, but a direction I am aiming towards. I tried writing letters to Mr Sutherland to say I had forgiven him. Last year, I even went back to the place where he had abused me and pronounced the forgiveness that I would have given him had I known what I do now. I prayed endlessly for God to help me to forgive him.

I have now come to a place where God knows I want to be separate from Mr Sutherland, and I do not want to hang on to what he did as my possession, but sometimes I have to struggle. I can still hardly bear to acknowledge the extent of his sin. The child who wants to believe he was acting for my good is still there, and if I am honest I can never fully forgive him until I have acknowledged his sin with all of myself.

22

At first I was so shocked about the amount of damage done to me emotionally that I could not even consider that what had happened had also damaged me in a spiritual way. For all the abused people I have talked to, there have been spiritual consequences. However, the exact nature of the damage varies depending on the details of the abuse. For myself, for example, I found the image of God as Father a very hard one to cope with.

From my childhood, my image of a father was of someone who was unable to cope with abuse, who could never know the details of it for fear of the consequences. Unwittingly I transferred this image on to God, and felt that I was unable to pray about the abuse. If God was my father then it all had to stay a secret. I also felt that, because my earthly father had such high expectations of me, I needed to work harder and do more all the time to please my heavenly Father too. If God was father, then he was remote and distant, a person to be pleased, rather than one who would delight in what he had created, whatever the imperfections. I have heard people who have been abused by their fathers saying that they can never even bear to think of God as a father like that. I have also, however, heard one woman say that she can only think of God as Father, since it was her own mother who abused her, and she finds refuge in the same image of God that I find so hard.

It is wrong to think that everyone is going to feel the same, and wrong to make any generalisations about images that will be helpful. Personally I find any reference to God or the Holy Spirit wanting to 'take control' of my life incredibly difficult. Although as an adult I want God to lead me in my life, the idea of control terrifies me. It is not an academic acceptance of what is meant by the words that I need, but a deep spiritual understanding, which I lack at the moment. I freeze inside when we sing descriptions of the work of the Holy Spirit as 'breaking, melting and moulding' or lyrics like 'Let the Holy Spirit come and take control'.

I am inwardly petrified of anyone taking control of me again. I have found in talking to other survivors that this is often a difficulty for them too. I want to be open to the work of God, but once I was open to a man who said that he loved me for what I was, a man who said he wanted my good – a man who was lying. I find it a major struggle to know that God is not a liar, that God will in no way abuse me. Rationally I know that God is far beyond any human image that we have, but sometimes I feel I cannot think past the experience. The idea of God abusing a person may seem such a wicked notion even to express, but in all honesty it is the heartfelt fear of some who have been abused.

It is a waste of time telling me that I have a distorted picture of God, the Holy Spirit, or Jesus – I *know* that, and pointing it out makes it worse! In fact, we all have a limited and distorted picture of the Trinity, and perhaps the areas I find so difficult are just more obvious to the onlooker. I speak from a place of damage and I know that I am not seeing things straight.

From my own experience I have found that I can relate in my prayers most openly to Jesus. I find the image of Christ incredibly helpful, and nowhere near as difficult as that of God or the Holy Spirit. However, it needs to be appreciated that anyone who was abused by their brother, for example, may have a different reaction. I love to read of the way Jesus treated women. I marvel at the way he was so opposite to others of his day. He valued women so highly. He spent a lot of time with them, and never used their vulnerability to overpower them. He had time for prostitutes, and was not afraid of sexual issues. He listened to women, and talked with them.

Christ also showed such a beautiful openness with children that he allays my fear of abuse. He said, 'Let the little children come to me' (Matt. 19:14). He did not force them, but he didn't want parents to hold their children back from him. He delighted in their innocence, and said that the kingdom of Heaven belonged to them. He did not despise their weakness; he did not abuse their simple trust. Instead he honoured it and used it as an example of greatness and wholeness. In everything, he was the opposite of an abuser. He loved the children for what they were and not for what he could get from them.

I have been told that I should be able to forgive Mr Sutherland, for Jesus said, 'For if you forgive men when they sin against you, your heavenly Father will also forgive you. But if you do not forgive men their sins, your Father will not forgive your sins' (Matt. 6:14). I appreciate that Jesus showed me the greatest example of forgiveness, and I find in him my hope for moving forward in this area. However, the same Jesus also took a child and said, 'And whoever welcomes a little child like this in my name welcomes me. But if anyone causes one of these little ones who believe in me to sin, it would be better for him to have a large millstone hung around his neck and to be drowned in the depths of the sea. Woe to the world because of the things that cause people to sin! Such things must come, but woe to the man through whom they come!' (Matt. 18:5–7.) I do not feel that this statement means I am exempt from moving towards forgiveness, but I delight in the fact that Jesus showed such understanding and sympathy for anything done to a child that might cause damage.

I also believe that Jesus suffered the ultimate abuse by his death on the cross. He can identify with the abused person's utter vulnerability, for he too was stretched out for everyone to see. Anyone could have done anything to him and violated him in any way. He knew what it was to be helpless, utterly dependent on the wishes of the people standing around. He showed in his death that, in order to reconcile each of us to God, he was prepared for such terrible abuse. I cannot imagine the pain or emotional and spiritual agony that Jesus went through. I know that I have only tasted a measure of it in my own experiences. I have found such comfort in knowing the truth of the words from Hebrews (4:15,16):

> Therefore, since we have a great high priest who has gone through the heavens, Jesus the Son of God, let us hold firmly to the faith we profess. For we do not have a high priest who is unable to sympathise with our weaknesses, but we have one who has been tempted in every way, just as we are – yet was without sin. Let us then approach the throne of grace with confidence, so that we may receive mercy and find grace to help us in our time of need.

I have spent so long struggling not to feel so awful about the areas in the Bible or images of God and the Holy Spirit that I find difficult. Now I have come to realise that although I have failed in many areas to understand the nature of God, so has everyone else! I have had a lot of pressure from other Christians to accept God as Father. They say this is fundamental, and I can hardly claim I have a relationship with God without this understanding. This, however, is simply untrue. I trust that in time my understanding of God will grow and develop, but at the moment it is not helpful to major on the areas of my faith that I find difficult. It is more important for me to build more on the areas I do not have a problem with.

I explained to someone once that I felt ashamed because I wanted the transforming work of the Holy Spirit in my life, but could not bear the way he was described. She pointed out something that may seem obvious, but was very helpful: there are other images of the Holy Spirit that may be easier to understand and may seem less threatening. What about the Bible picture of the Holy Spirit coming as a dove, for example? Why hadn't I thought about that? I had become so terrified by the images usually put forward by the Church that I had forgotten that the Holy Spirit does not only come in ways that may be described as 'overpowering'.

I heard a preacher recently describe the intimate way in which God wants to be your lover'. I know what he meant, but the very words made me physically sick and the tears just flowed down my face in grief at the very idea. To anyone who knows nothing about abuse, I may seem quite awful not to want that intimate relationship. It isn't the relationship that I don't want – it is the terminology that I find so difficult. When I tried explaining this to a church leader, he exclaimed that I was asking him to preach half a gospel. Far be it from me to try to do such a thing. All I am asking is that if you do preach or teach, try to understand that for some in your congregation these concepts may be difficult. If you are working with the abused, do not force them along the path that may seem universally right.

I am coming to a broader understanding the more I am counselled and the more I come to terms with the abuse. If all the time the pressure is on for me to change my attitude, I end up feeling increasingly useless and even more different from other Christians. I had not realised for a long time why it was that I found some parts of the service so hard, or why I couldn't bear to sing some of the songs. Now that I have understood why, it has taken away a lot of the shame and I feel less 'odd'.

I have also struggled considerably with praying. I find it comparatively easy to pray for others, but I am not very good at sitting still on my own, as you will have gathered. However, I have discovered that I can pray as I walk with the pram, or rock the little ones. I pray in the bath, as I wash up, as I change the nappies. These are the times when I can pray for the many needs of other people.

I have found it very hard to be alone and pray about myself. The image I have had of myself has been so poor that I have felt I cannot bear to come before a God who I have felt would just condemn me, although that is not true. For many years I was scared to be alone. All I could do would be to sit and cry, and I knew there were no words that I could pray with. Now I am learning that God knows every tear, and the cause of them, and now I sit and offer my tears to God in prayer. I have even had to resort to typing out a letter to God. Somehow, at times of great depression, I can hardly bring myself to say the words. I know that I have missed out on so much in my relationship with God. Now, with more counselling and support, this is changing, but I thought it important to indicate how far-reaching the effects of abuse really are.

23

If I could give one message to the church I am part of in this country, I would ask it to stop being so naïve about abuse. There is an understandable but misinformed view that such things could not possibly happen within the Church. We may concede that there are men and women who are now talking about abuse that happened in the past, but there is a general reticence to accept that the same thing is still happening. It is time we woke up to the stark reality that in our congregations there are people who are currently being abused. There are men and women worshipping with us who are abusing their own children, or others in their care.

When surveys have been done to assess the extent of damage both past and present, we would like to think that in the Church the statistics of abuse are at least lower. Unfortunately, at best, they are the same as the rest of society. At worst, we may have to acknowledge that since abuse flourishes in closed groups, there may be more happening under the surface in churches than we realise. Recent cases of religious leaders found guilty of sexually abusing children for a number of years have resulted in many other people coming forward and saying that abuse has happened to them, but they previously have not felt they would have been believed.

Now we are in a climate where people will listen, where the clergy and leaders are being held accountable, more is coming out into the open. We must face reality, and start dealing with the fact that anyone can abuse. There are no particular requirements of social or economic background, no particular age or stage of life. Abusers come in all shapes and sizes, and virtually always, when they are discovered, everyone exclaims they never thought that person would ever do such a thing! If we took this seriously, we would start to put into operation measures that would expose abuse in its earliest stages. By ignoring the reality of the situation, we are in danger of encouraging abuse to flourish.

To start with, think how infrequently, if at all, words like abuse are even used in church teaching. It seems to be such a taboo issue that the word is not even mentioned. It is not enough to speak vaguely about sexual immorality. Someone who abuses may be under the delusion that children enjoy this kind of behaviour and may not even consider it as being sinful. The Church has the responsibility to enlighten them. Sexual abuse must be named as a sin and a criminal activity. I have heard the account of Amnon and Tamar (2 Sam. 13) preached about as a story of man's greed; I have heard about the damage of sin in the life of Amnon after he had acted improperly. I have heard that story described in many different ways, but never have I heard the correct description of incest being used. In one verse of the story, Tamar is described after the abuse as being 'a desolate woman' (v. 20). I have never heard a reference to what we should learn from her side of the story.

If you can absorb the amount of damage done by abuse you might understand why it is so important that it is talked about within the Church. If the subject is not discussed, the abuser might wrongly assume that what he or she is doing does not come within the scope of the Church. The abused person feels more isolated, since it feels as if the Church is becoming part of the secret that he or she is trying to have exposed.

One minister in our local area was involved in the healing process of a young woman who had been abused. He had no idea of the large number of people who have been abused. On one Sunday he began to preach, and mentioned abuse. Within a week, eleven people had come to him and secretly confided that they, too, had been abused. Since he had publicly declared that there was a problem with abuse, those people had felt that perhaps the Church was, after all, somewhere to find help and some kind of healing.

Recently I asked to speak in our church about the conference I had attended. The majority of people in our church do not know that I have been abused, and this was the first time I was able to state publicly the high proportion of people who have suffered abuse. In the congregation there was a young woman who had been abused. She was not a Christian, but had come searching for some kind of way through the terrible pain she was experiencing as she grappled with her past. After I had spoken, she was in tears. It was only the second Sunday she had come to church. She then said to me 'All these years I have kept away from church because I never thought that they talked about that sort of thing. I didn't feel that I had any right to come because I have been abused. I cannot believe that you can talk about it here.' I didn't like to tell this young woman that I had been in the church for seventeen years, and it was the first time it had ever been mentioned publicly!

We need also to scrutinise carefully our teaching of the children in our churches. We are in danger of giving unhelpful messages in our attempts to bring children to God. I have heard great emphasis on children always needing to obey and be good. When the children are in the main service I rarely hear mention that adults also do things wrong, and that adults are also answerable for all their actions. We encourage the family unit, where parents are in charge and children blindly obey. Obedience has become paramount, and discipline a sign of good Christian parents.

I would never want to go to the extreme of saying all this is wrong, but I want to point out that there are times when children may say 'no'. Parents can help by telling their children they do not have to do things to make an adult feel happy when they think their body is being abused. The Church needs to support parents in giving the same message. I have never heard it said publicly that there are any exceptions to obedience, thus we have taken away our children's only means of self-defence. We must put far more energy into telling children they are of value to God, and into showing them by our lives and treatment of them the value we also place on them. We need to convey that each child has rights, and can make demands for proper care and attention. If as a Church we fail to make children feel special, we are exposing them to abuse.

Think of what would happen if, for example, a child in your church says that he or she is being abused by the Youth Worker. Who would you believe? Would you even listen long enough to check out the story? Would the child be able to express how he or she was made to feel uncomfortable? Sadly, the more likely scenario is that we would think that the child was lying. We would not be able to believe that our dear Christian brother or sister could ever do such a thing. You only have to read endless accounts of people who have been abused to realise that very often they did tell someone about it and they were either told off or disbelieved. This served to close them up completely and the damage was further intensified.

I know that the thought of someone in our church being accused of sexual abuse is ghastly. Which of us would ever want to be involved with dealing with it? However, we must not make the mistake of thinking it is a sin that can be quietly dealt with by the church leadership. It is not minor, and it is likely to be repeated, so the abuser needs help as well as the abused. So often our instinct is to meet and talk with the abuser, and to relax when we see tears of penitence and even a public apology. This is not enough, and if the church fails to acknowledge that a crime has been committed, then we are in danger of acting as accomplices.

Does this mean that having contacted Social Services or the police, we then have nothing more to do with the abuser? By no means. If we are to act to change the situation, then we will support the abuser to face the public result of his or her sin. Support them, love them, show any amount of care for them that you can, but if you really do love and care you will let them come face to face with the consequences of their actions. If there is a case of incest within the church, then the whole family will need support. Be on your guard against giving all the attention to the penitent abuser who is probably making more noise than the quieter victim. The damage done to the victim will last all his or her life. The church and the parents of the child need to give the same message to the child:

First, a terrible sin has been committed against you. You were not in the wrong. You were not to blame. The responsibility for all that has happened lies entirely with the person who abused you.

Second, you were right to tell. It was a brave and difficult thing to do. It is not your fault that now there are far-reaching consequences, even to the extent that your own family has been broken up. This is not your fault.

Third, we will support you, now and in the future. The effects of what has happened will not go away immediately, and we understand that.

Sadly, one likely consequence of abuse, and particularly incest, is that the family may be broken up. The innocent partner may not feel able to maintain the marriage relationship in the face of the nature of the sin. It is too easy for the Church to give glib and easy answers, saying that couples should always stay together, and this can be seen as underestimating the sin that has been committed. If, for example, a man in the church had raped a woman, we would not be so eager to seek for reconciliation in their relationship. Yet when the same thing happens to a child we try to carry on as if nothing too serious has happened. We may feel that we are seeking to protect the child, but in reality we are adding to the damage done. The child is unable to speak for himself or herself, and may not be able to express his or her feelings coherently for many years.

Instead of blurring the issues, the Church, in its actions and words, must show who is innocent and who is guilty.

We could take the reasonable precaution of having police checks on everyone working with young people or children, including creches. This may seem excessive, but the Church aims to teach love and trust. Are we really loving our children if we are allowing them to be exposed to someone who has come into church claiming to be seeking after God? Men and women who are sincere Christians have abused children. We have still not grasped the implication of the words in 1 Samuel 16:7: 'The LORD does not look at the things man looks at. Man looks at the outward appearance, but the LORD looks at the heart.' So often we are frightened to accept the implications for our church communities. We act as if we would always be able to tell who an abuser was, even though all the evidence says this is unlikely. If you look at the average church library, you can see that people are struggling with many problems, but would there be anything to help the one in four women, or the one in twelve men, who have been sexually abused?

If a church does start to deal with abused people as adults, it will come across all sorts of difficulties, and might secretly wish it had never started to talk about the subject! As you can tell from my own account, people who are trying to come to terms with abuse may present all kinds of problems in their relationships with those in church. I have found that if a counselling session has been particularly deep, I am much more emotionally vulnerable for a few days. This has meant that on the Sunday following the session I may be much worse at coping with looking at anyone or being touched. At these times, I want to get into church and out again with as little contact as possible. Some people obviously find this difficult. Most weeks I am outgoing and receptive, and it is hard for others to know how to react when I am different. I am embarrassed at the way I am on these days, and often I am tempted to stay at home and not bother with the struggle. However, I feel I have to go and meet with others, however difficult it is, because when I am at my lowest ebb then their fellowship and love matters even more than when I feel all right. I would ask, then, that you do not hastily judge the behaviour or attitudes of anyone you know, or suspect, has been abused. They are already struggling with those aspects of their personality that are less than socially acceptable. The censure of others only serves to make them feel worse, or confirms their inner feeling that they are no use anyway.

I have been told by one inexperienced leader that he was concerned because I obviously had a poor attitude towards men. Even though he knew about the abuse, he said he felt that I seemed very rebellious and quite unwilling to be told what to do at times. I had to learn to submit, he said, and this would help in my healing from the memories of abuse. It did not seem to occur to him that what he saw as rebelliousness was a self-protective reaction coming from a terrible fear. He may spend a long time trying to tell me I am wrong, praying for me to see the right way. What I need him to say is that he finds that aspect of me difficult, but accepts it. Perhaps with more understanding on the part of leaders, it would not be so difficult to think they were worth obeying. I am not saying that someone who is abused is exempt from correction, or that all they do is as a consequence of their abuse, but there are many aspects that are, and these are not sins – they are natural responses to deep pain.

Many people over the years have quoted Scriptures at me, and told me to learn them and quote them every time I find something hard. I love the word of God and believe that within it there is healing. However, I've found that those who use quotes out of context prove quite unhelpful. One person told me that whenever I had a bad thought about my abuser, or if I was depressed, I had to think of the verse in Philippians 4:8: 'Whatever is true, whatever is noble, whatever is right, whatever is pure, whatever is lovely, whatever is admirable – if anything is excellent or praiseworthy – think about such things.' I tried it. I had it stuck up on my kitchen wall. I learned the verse, and tried to be positive. No matter how bad things were, I struggled to look at the good side. Then the professional counsellor said I had spent so much time looking at the good things, trying to think about all the lovely aspects of my abuser, that I failed to comprehend the awfulness of what he had done. It was easier, in a way, to look always at the positive side of everything. It was more painful, but absolutely necessary, to look at the negative side too, but which Christian tells you to think about the sin and the dark side? We talk instead only of victory and healing. Having dealt with the negative, then maybe it is possible to emerge and dwell on the beautiful, but we should not misuse our faith to repress emotions that should be faced. God seems well able to love someone who hates, someone who struggles, someone who is doubting, and it is a shame that Christians sometimes offer love that is conditional. The abused person must be told and shown that they are of value, not just for what they might be, but for what they are. I did not need loads of programmes to help me towards recovery. I needed, first, a counsellor who had a much wider grasp of the area of sexual abuse to help me change some of the feelings in a helpful and supportive way. Second, I needed love from ordinary, unqualified people who seemed somehow to like me, even if I was erractic in my behaviour. People who could come alongside my pain and let me share some of their own were the ones who helped me most, as were those who did not have agendas for what a perfect Christian was. Once anyone can reach the point of accepting themselves as they are, then they are freer to develop and become more whole. But all the while they are struggling to reach the next stage, the striving in itself can take away their ability to be healed – it can be self-defeating. I now love the scripture that says, 'Be still and know that I am God' (Ps. 46:10). That promises a place of no strife, no yearning to be someone else, but a real acceptance of who we are and who God is.

I am not suggesting that everyone in the church should focus on those who have been abused and force them to talk about their experiences. The abused person should be allowed to take control of the decision of whom to tell. They should be allowed to disclose as much or as little as they want to. If we force them to tell more and more when they are not ready, we are in danger of abusing their emotions and compounding their problems. My best friends have been those who have allowed me to talk at my own rate and who, amazingly, have never seemed bored or uninterested, even when I have felt the need to go over the same ground again.

Talking about abuse, or listening to someone else, may be difficult, and since sexual abuse has been a taboo area for so long, we do not always know how to react appropriately. Speaking for myself, what others have said has often seemed relatively unimportant; the more I have talked, the more I have come to absorb what happened to me.

In listening without judgement you become a major part of someone's healing. Allow them to seek change at the speed they are able to cope with, but do not demand that they change. Sexual abuse has damaged their emotions so severely that the only thing you can be sure of is that it will be a long-term commitment.

When I announced that I was setting up a survivors' group in our church for anyone in the area who had been abused, one lady came up and said, 'Well, I haven't been abused, but I would gladly make the tea for you.' This was so much more supportive than the person who said that they couldn't see the point of a lot of people with distorted pictures of God getting together, because they would never see things clearly!

There are ways of responding to someone who has been abused that are more helpful than others. Personally I find it difficult to look straight at people when I have a bad day. I lower my eyes because somehow I feel safer. If someone looked straight at me, then I would feel they could see my inner pain and I cannot cope with that. At these times I also find it hard if someone tries to hold my hand or put their arm round me. Although part of me wants to be held, I shy away from physical touch when I am struggling emotionally.

When the part of the service comes when people are encouraged to 'give the peace', this can be a nightmare. Sometimes we say the Grace at the end of a service and we are told to look at each other and address each other with the prayer. This is fine in theory, but for me it is an invitation to internal panic. The fear rises inside me until all I want to do is run from the church and never go back. The most helpful response to this is acceptance. I do not feel happy at the way I am responding, but rejecting myself, or feeling the rejection of others, only makes it worse. I have learned a technique now that means I offer my blessing to the bowl of flowers on bad days, or maybe the hymn numbers – that feels less threatening than people! Someone once remarked, as I sat down after the prayer having not looked round like the rest of the congregation, 'Well, I hope your back enjoyed that blessing!' I felt wrongly humiliated and ashamed.

Ask anyone who has been abused and they will give you their own list of things, they struggle with, and they are often areas that seem very simple to others. I can, for example, stand up and speak in church from behind a lectern, but I cannot take the offering. I feel that when I do this everyone can just look at my body, and I feel vulnerable and frightened. What is the point of forcing myself to take the offering as a kind of penance for my weakness? I am now at the stage where I thank God I can stand behind the lectern, and I shall leave someone else to take the offering! I am having to learn to accept my emotional limitations, although in time they may change. I am beginning to realise that I do walk, as it were, with an 'emotional limp'. However, I am still part of the body of Christ and I need to be able to find acceptance within it.

24

The conference was over and I arrived back at the station, relieved that I had found my way through the narrow side streets of the city. It had been a brilliant day, but I was really tired now. The train was crowded and I had difficulty finding a seat, but once I had found a corner to sit in, I was able to lose myself in reflections on the day. I hoped that I had not chosen a seat next to someone who would chatter all the way home. I was so glad of the chance to think, and I knew that when I got home I would not easily get that opportunity.

There had been about two hundred people at the conference, and I was amazed how different everyone's backgrounds were. One aspect struck me with particular force. While I was listening to one speaker, I noticed a woman crying. Her husband had gone with her to the conference, and as she cried he lovingly stroked her shoulder and offered her his handkerchief. I looked at his face, and was shocked at the pain in his eyes.

It made me think about how little I had considered the hurt that my abuse had caused Peter. Somehow it is always the person who is abused who goes for counselling and receives support, and yet the partner must be experiencing all sorts of emotions. Where had he been able to go for help? How had he managed to cope with my mood swings and unpredictability? He has somehow had to learn to respond appropriately to my times of severe depression. In many ways he has paid the price of my being abused over and over again.

I remembered the time that we both read the books on holiday in Scotland, and how he cried with me. What happened to his grief? Has he been able to make any more sense of what is happening in our marriage and in my personality than I have?

I have always turned to him expecting him to be there for me always. I have blamed him if he has been less than 100 per cent supportive and understanding of each stage I have been through. He has been so faithful, and has always tried to be the caring husband I have needed.

Sitting in that train, I wished that I had been less selfish and thought more of the effects of it all on Peter's life. He did not even know anything about the abuse when he married me, and had to cope first with severe sexual difficulties, and then with the bombshell of what had happened to the woman he loved when she was a child. He had no friends who were close enough to confide in about his inner feelings – he has had to handle everything alone.

If I could have the time again I would try and think more about how hard it must be for partners of abused people. I have since met other partners, and realise that the importance of this area has been severely underestimated. We should be doing something to ensure that partners get any help or support that they need. Usually the last person who can help them is the partner who has been abused, for they are too preoccupied trying to make sense of their own tangle.

Since that time I have sought to listen to other people's partners, and I have discovered that one thing in common is that they are very often completely overwhelmed by the sudden rush of forces and emotions from their partner, which previously they knew nothing about. From being in a fairly predictable situation, and thinking that they knew the person they had married, they suddenly have a whole new dynamic which seems to be out of control and completely impossible to discuss with anyone. Many have expressed their desire to be very supportive, but honestly don't know what to do for the best.

The inner emotions that were uncovered when I came to deal with the abuse were new to me, but they were also fresh to Peter, and I wrongly expected him to have ready answers to questions we were both only just beginning to ask. I had scarcely acknowledged the extreme anger that Peter must feel towards Mr Sutherland for abusing me, or even towards my parents for not handling the situation better. I felt ashamed that I had not also listened to his feelings, which he had hardly been able to share with me, knowing that I was so angry myself.

How difficult it must be for partners in cases of incest, when they have become related to those who have damaged the person they love. One man shared the fact that he had lost a lot of confidence when he handled or cuddled his own children. His wife, who had been abused as a child had so lost trust in anyone touching the children that he felt he was always under surveillance and had abandoned normal, healthy games of tickling and cuddling since he was frightened his wife would view things differently.

'How we all need to talk with each other more,' I mused half-aloud, and then blushed as I realised where I was. Fortunately, the lady next to me had fallen asleep. I closed my eyes to keep up my welcome isolation and carried on thinking.

The day had been such a busy one, but so profitable. I had realised that what I had thought was a private battle with my own inner forces was in fact something that had far wider implications. What on earth should the Church be doing about people who had been abused, were being abused, or who were abusing others? It would be a lot easier to think about how dismally the Church had failed to take the problems seriously and had even unwittingly perpetuated some, but then I realised with a sinking feeling that, as a follower of Christ, I was part of the Church and I too had responsibility in this area. If the Church has failed to understand some of the issues, maybe I have failed to try to convey them.

Where or how can we all begin to work in a positive way towards the change that we want to see? To start with, we should acknowledge that we each have a vital role to play in the slow process of change. Since I have been abused, I have the unique chance of explaining things that I would not have understood otherwise. However, my views cannot be prescriptive for others, and it is only now, after a lot of counselling, that I can even begin to think about wider issues. People who have not been abused still have responsibility in this area, and they need to work alongside the abused, maybe to express those things that the abused have little energy left to fight for because of their own attempts to sort out their feelings.

However difficult it is, no matter how daunting the task appears, the Church needs to speak out on behalf of the children who are otherwise forced to be silent. Who else is going to take this responsibility? Society in general has not really undertaken to protect children enough. The leaders of the nation are cutting funding to many of the caring services, with the effect that there are fewer facilities offering help to someone who has been abused. Voluntary organisations are carrying the main responsibility for helping people, and the Church must play a leading role. We need to be involved in politics so that we can encourage the government of our day to take responsibility in this area. Then we must be prepared to fund projects and groups who are seeking to address the problem and to support the abused and their families. One person who is very concerned with helping abused people told me that he has been involved with fund-raising for various Christian projects. He said that people will willingly give to projects for homeless people and drug addicts, for example, but often do not understand the need to help people who have been abused. Since they have no visible handicap, they are not perceived as needing help. Information and education are the only ways we can hope to change this attitude.

We must try to ensure that church leaders are educated as part of their training, so that they are more equipped to help. Many clergy I have spoken to say that they were not prepared in any way by their training for the problems relating to abuse. This is something they have had to learn as they went along, and one can hardly blame them for some of the mistakes made en route. I feel, however, that a word of reservation is needed here. I have been counselled quite extensively by two pastors and this seemed at the time to be part of God's provision for me, and it was just that. None the less, although they did their best and gave so sacrificially of themselves, I have to acknowledge that I might have been helped more quickly and with less pain by people who knew more about the subject.

Leaders must learn at what level they are able to help, and at what stage they should refer the person on to someone else. A minister who is doing a job of caring for the whole church will not have the time, the training, or the emotional strength to cope with the long-term demands of helping someone to be healed from the effects of sexual abuse. They are qualified and experienced ministers, and although they can do some counselling, they are not counsellors either in profession or training. Professional counsellors must be supervised, but they can offer a detachment that is helpful and healing and they are able to be far more single-minded in the help that they give.

This is not a failure on the part of ministers, but we are not helping anyone if there is pressure on the clergy to be over-involved with people in need of deep healing in this or any other area. Ministers are often very isolated, and can be limited in their pastoral role. The process can be very confusing for the minister and the counsellee, and often there are seriously conflicting interests. If someone else is able to take over this role, then the minister is freed to pastor the whole church and not just a few of the congregation. When I was being counselled by the pastor I could never go to him with any other difficulties without them being seen in the context of the abuse and the panic attacks. I was not, therefore, as free to develop spiritually as I might have been. My own experience leads me to conclude that I needed both a pastor and a counsellor – no one person could be both.

I would advise ministers that they are in an excellent position to talk initially to someone about the abuse. They can then come alongside that person and help him or her to move on to get the necessary help. Having got the person to the place where he or she can receive professional counselling, the pastor is then freed to support the person through the inevitably long process ahead. This may seem like a rejection to the abused person, but it may be the kindest and most supportive thing that a minister can do. Ministers therefore need to ensure that they know what provision there is locally, so that they can refer people to appropriate agencies.

You are most likely to discover that there are many secular groups doing an excellent job of offering help, but there are never enough. Churches need to become local resources themselves, but this is only possible with more education and understanding and a great deal of communication with existing agencies. If nothing else, we can work alongside these groups by at least letting them use church premises that would otherwise remain locked.

I was surprised by how many people there were at the conference who had not been abused, having wrongly assumed that only people who had experienced abuse would care enough to do anything about it. I doubt that most abused people would need any persuading about what I have written. Most probably, they will passionately want to do anything to prevent the same thing from happening to someone else. However, since they are often struggling themselves, they also need people who have not been abused to campaign and change things. By working together and listening to each other more, we will be able to see the Church demonstrating the value that God places on the life of every individual.

Having acknowledged that we should not expect church leaders to provide the deep counselling people may need, and having accepted that, once unleashed, the needs are extensive, we then have to work at getting far more people trained as counsellors. While I accept that men can be abused as well as women, we have to admit that statistically this is less likely. It is not helpful to counsel people of the opposite sex in areas relating to abuse – the issues are so deep and so complex. I had not appreciated how much easier it was to talk to a woman, having previously only talked to a man, albeit a very sensitive and helpful one. I found that when I was with a woman in a counselling situation I did not feel panic at all, and the fear of being emotionally manipulated was gone. This made it so much easier to move towards healing.

We need to make it easier for women to train, possibly funding them and at least encouraging them, so that there is greater provision for women who need to come to terms with their past. It is not enough just to sympathise and pour tea: we need to help people with much more insight than that, given the extent of the damage.

For too long Christians have been content to go for the cheapest, quickest form of help, and now we need to raise our standards of counselling. The Association of Christian Counsellors has been set up to accredit Christians in counselling in the pastoral and community setting, and they assess training for recognition at Basic, Advanced, and Specialist levels. These standards are nationally recognised and are comparable with the British Association of Counselling. As the courses become increasingly widespread, the Church should support the Association and train as many people as possible. Training is lengthy, but if we don't start soon we will never get out of the present situation.

One big problem many face when they feel they need to go for professional counselling is that they simply cannot afford it. In my own case I had been unable to go for psychotherapy at an early stage, even if I had wanted to, because we were already struggling with two young children, one salary, and a large mortgage. While the Church may be unable to offer any alternative counselling, it may at least be able to find ways of financially supporting the counselling that someone needs, either partly or wholly. In some areas of America the abuser is made to pay the cost of therapy for the person they abused.

Counselling is not to be seen as an optional extra: it is the only way for someone to get the help that they need. In some Christian circles it is even considered less spiritual to receive such help, and it is implied that with more faith, or a better understanding of Scripture, the problem could be sorted out. We think nothing about people going for physiotherapy for broken limbs, but we expect people with broken hearts to get up and walk without any further fuss or professional help. I do not find it wrong for the Church to say that within its normal structure it cannot meet the needs of these people – what is worse is when they feel that they can meet the needs, then fail to encourage the person to go where they might really be helped.

There may be times when it is easier to ignore what is happening and there are many areas that need to be reformed, of which abuse is only one, but we have to start somewhere. We are called to influence the communities in which God has placed us. We need to address issues that others may find uncomfortable. The Church needs to speak for the children who are being abused today, and it needs to hear and help those who were abused yesterday.

It had been a long journey and I had done a lot of thinking about the broader issues of abuse while the train rattled along. Stimulated by the conference, I was ready for action and enthusiastic about change. I was almost prepared to jump up on the seat and call everyone else in the carriage to action. The more I thought about the exciting role the Church could play, the keener I was about going home to begin to work in this direction. I looked round the carriage, but the nodding heads and sleepy eyes indicated that no one else seemed to be thinking about such wide-ranging issues! The man opposite me was obviously bored with his journey, and when he saw me looking round for the first time in two hours he decided to engage in conversation.

'Have you been to York for a visit, or are you going somewhere else?' he ventured.

'I've just been to a conference,' I replied. 'Have you been somewhere interesting?'

'No, I've been to the dullest wedding in ages, and I'm glad it's over.'

I didn't know exactly what the appropriate response was, so I half laughed and hoped that was right.

'What was the conference about?' he carried on.

For an instant I wished that I had been to a conference on

any other subject. 'It was about child sexual abuse and the Church's response,' I replied, looking at him as directly as I could so that he would not think I was embarrassed by his question; carrying on, I said, 'You see, the Church really needs to be leading the nation in this direction – it is really interesting, I have had a brilliant day.'

I noticed a few pairs of eyes turn in my direction and it was obvious that those around had eavesdropped on our conversation.

The man shifted in his seat, and his blush betrayed that he wished he hadn't asked in the first place.

I smiled at him as reassuringly as I knew how – abuse was no longer a subject to be kept secret or neglected. I for one am committed, along with many others, to making sure that it will not be hidden in the future.

The train lurched to a sudden stop at the station, and there was Peter on the platform with the children.

I was glad to be home.

Postscript

If you have read this book with the hope that someone is going to offer you a sure or quick route to healing the pain caused by abuse, I am afraid you will have been sadly disappointed. I could spend a lot of time telling you how much *more* healing is needed in my life. Even the most unobservant will have realised that at times I am still grieving and angry, still moving towards a complete forgiveness. Maybe you feel that I should not publish a book until I am more whole.

I would love to write an ending that says I have complete peace about all that has happened, and I am now a victorious Christian woman walking into the sunset with my neat answers alongside me. I am afraid that my experience has not meant that I can honestly write that. One thing I have discovered is that there are no neat answers, but lots of deep, hard questions that will not be answered entirely this side of eternity.

I have also discovered that the way I view my situation depends on which way I look at things. When I look at the areas of my life that still need changing, when I analyse things I still find difficult, then I could despair and think that I will never be any different. However, if I look back and consider how far I have come, then I can begin to rejoice in the measure of healing I have already received. In spite of everything, or maybe because of it, I am happily married, and have five gorgeous children (our fifth child arrived halfway through the recent years of counselling). I am able to work part-time as a teacher. I can still function in church, even though sometimes it is hard. I can dress in attractive clothes and not try to hide my shape. I can use make-up. There are many times when I am happy and able to function really well, both for myself, and as a wife and mother.

Life is full of varied and enjoyable experiences now, and in reality abuse no longer dominates me as it once did. Yet I do still get bouts of bad depression, and at those times I grieve once again, and sometimes that makes me go through the stage of acute anger once more. I am now seeing a professional counsellor to try to sort out areas that I still have not been able to face.

I was once ashamed that I needed help from others to such an extent. Now I have come to realise that I will need help for a while to come, so that I can keep on the path to further healing. I go to a woman who has had many years experience of counselling, and who knows far more about abuse and the consequences than most people would.

I have spent so many years struggling for wholeness, striving to be something different. I have tried so hard to hide the emotional limp that I walk with. I have been to meetings and asked for healing. I have had hands laid on, and have been prayed for endlessly. I have read the Scriptures searching for the solution. I have been to so many meetings, got involved in so many activities, anything to dull the pain and feel that I am no longer damaged.

I referred earlier to Joni Eareckson, who has come to a place of acceptance of her paralysis and her need for a wheelchair. Now I am coming to the same place in emotional terms. Yes, I am damaged, and know that in some areas I act inappropriately, and do not look like the 'victorious Christian woman' others expect to see.

I am what I am, though. I cannot struggle and strive as though by screaming louder and more angrily God will heal me. For whatever reason, I still experience some of the damaging after-effects of abuse. I am now trying to learn to glorify God within the limits of this handicap, rather than fighting against who I am and trying to force myself to be someone else. God assures me that he loves me just as I am. I know this is not the end to the story, but I cannot wait for ever to explain what is happening. It is so easy to clutch at stories of Christians who have been miraculously healed and – if our experience is anything less than this – to feel lacking in faith or less holy. I am still an unhealed Christian, and that is an all right person to be! I have been damaged, but, thank God, I have definitely not been destroyed.

One particular experience I had made a tremendous impact on the way I have viewed the after-effects of abuse. One night while I was being counselled, the anger that I felt was so strong it was becoming all-consuming. Now, I know in my head that everything that happens to us God will use for our good. I can accept that nothing I have experienced is going to be lost in his eternal plan. Sometimes, though, I feel as if from this side of eternity the loss I have experienced is so major that God could not possibly do what he has promised.

On this particular night I was thinking back to the time when I sat at the typewriter on the very first evening that I tried to sort out my fear of needles. I realise now that what really hit me then was the much deeper feelings about the abuse that the needle phobia had been hiding. The very memory of rushing out of the house and going into such a terrible panic attack was still so painful, that I could hardly bear to remember it, never mind the experiences that had led up to it. On this night, though, I was thinking about what would have happened if I had stayed in the room and not run out. I was trying to lose the intervening years in my mind, and wanting to express to God my anger at what I felt were just wasted years. In my heart I desperately wished that God had taken away the pain at that moment. I struggled with the fact that emotional problems are virtually never healed in an instant.

As I prayed and expressed all this anger before God, I could see the lounge and myself quite clearly. I could see piles and piles of wasted and broken experiences. All there seemed to be was mess and destruction. In the middle of everything there stood a treasure box. I did not want to open it, because I feared that once the lid was off it would be like dealing with the abuse – impossible to get everything back in again.

I asked God to transform the memory of the pain I had

experienced dealing with the abuse. As I opened the lid, the damage had all gone and inside were the most beautiful jewels and other priceless and precious items. The box was crammed full of them, and I handled them all with delight.

Seeing this picture helped to change how I felt about the past. For one moment I had a glimpse of what things might look like from eternity. There could be no denial of the things that had happened; everything was there in the box. But in some amazing way, God had transformed all the ugliness into something that was beautiful. It is hard to express in words how that picture has strengthened me. Yes, at the moment it sometimes feels as if I am walking through a derelict bomb site, but I now have a deeper understanding and I believe that ultimately I will be united with a God who has seen all that has happened and has used everything to become a 'treasure in his hand'.

Material that you might find helpful

Books

A Silence to be Broken by Earl D. Wilson (IVP, Leicester, 1986).

Breaking Through by Kathy Ann Matthews (Albatross, London, 1990).

Child Sexual Abuse by Maxine Hancock and Karen Burton Mains (Highland Books, Sussex, 1988).

Christianity and Child Sexual Abuse by Hilary Cashman (SPCK, London, 1993).

Cry Hard and Swim by Jacqueline Spring (Virago, London, 1988).

Feeling Happy, Feeling Safe by Michele Elliot (colouring book for ages 3–7) (Hodder Headline, London, 1991).

Intended for Pleasure by Ed and Gaye Wheat (Scripture Union, London, 1977).

Keeping Safe: A practical Guide to Talking with Children by Michele Elliot (Hodder Headline, London, 1994).

Recovery from Abuse: Bible Study Guide by Dale and Juanita Ryan (Scripture Union, London, 1992).

Relate Guide to Sex in Loving Relationships by Sarah Litvinoff (Vermilion, London, 1993).

Seven for a Secret by Tracy Hansen (Triangle, London, 1991).

Sexual Assault and Abuse: A Handbook for Clergy and Religious Professionals ed. by Mary D Pellauer, Barbara Chester and Jane Boyajian (Harper, San Francisco, 1987).

The Courage to Heal by Ellen Bass and Laura Davis (Cedar: Octopus, London, 1992).

The Wounded Heart by Dr Dan B. Allender (CWR, Surrey, 1991).

When You've Been Abused, A Reason for Hope Series (Here's Life Publishers, Milton Keynes, 1986).

Training packs

Protecting Children: Training Pack for Front-line Carers (HMSO, 1992).

Taking Care: A Church Response to Children, Adults and Abuse (National Children's Bureau, 1992).

Videos

Cosmo and Dibs Keep Safe (ages 3–6) (BBC and Kidscape).

Frozen Peas: Healing the Memories of Childhood Sexual Abuse by Linda Caine (Sunrise Video).

Now I Can Tell You My Secret (ages 8–11) (Walt Disney and Kidscape).

Where to go for help

There are some organisations that have bases throughout the country. You can find their addresses and telephone numbers in the local telephone directory, e.g.:

Social Services Department
NSPCC (National Society for Prevention of Cruelty to Children)
Family Service Units (some areas only)
Probation Service (not Scotland)
Family Welfare Association
Samaritans
Citizens' Advice Bureau
MIND

A very useful resource for further addresses is:
The Survivors' Directory 1994. This is a directory of support services for survivors of sexual violence in Britain and Ireland. Regularly updated, it contains over 300 addresses and phone numbers. It includes: counselling services for adult survivors; counselling services for male survivors; supported accommodation; services for abusers; services for children and their parents; training and support for workers.

It is produced by:
Broadcasting Support Services
Victoria House
21 Manor Street
Ardwick
Manchester
M12 6HE

Other addresses
This list covers a wide spectrum of viewpoints and, although

each organisation has agreed to its inclusion at the end of this book, it does not necessarily agree with the views expressed within it, and neither would the author agree with all the approaches offered by these different groups.

Association of Christian Counsellors: Training agency; trains counsellors in both the Christian and secular field; all aspects of counselling including sexual abuse.
Roger and Glenyss Altman
St Clears Road
Johnstown
Carmarthen
Dyfed SA32 3HH
0267 230428

Barnabas House Christian Centre: Residential accommodation for adults who have been abused as children; team of trained counsellors available; literature for those who have been abused.
  Address as for **Association of Christian Counsellors**.

Beacon Foundation: A Christian organisation that has been set up to help professionals and church members to have a better understanding of the problems caused by witchcraft, Satanism, and ritual abuse.
3 Grosvenor Avenue
Rhyl
Clwyd
LL18 4HA

Boarding School Survivors (BSS): For anyone who found elements of life at boarding school abusive in any way; self-help groups; workshops and counselling for families and friends.
128A Northview Road
London
N8 7LP
081 341 4885

Campaign Against Pornography (CAP): Membership-based organisation to raise public awareness of national pornography and campaigning against the pornography industry. It receives many calls from people who have been sexually abused where pornography has been included. Referral service for further help; national network; support group (London only) for women escaping from or suffering in the sex industry.
11 Goodwin Street
London N4 3HQ
071 263 1833

Catholic Marriage Advisory Council: To provide relationship preparation for marriage and family life; relationship counselling for all adults, not just Catholics; contact national number for local group.
Clitherow House
1 Blythe Road
London W14 ONW
071 371 1341

Child Abuse Survivors Network: National organisation formed to help survivors of any form of maltreatment in childhood. The initial aim is to generate information and communication and to help shed light on the problems and needs of abuse survivors; newsletters; penfriends' scheme; not a helpline.
PO Box 1
London N1 7SN
071 278 8414

Childline: Childline will talk to any child about any problem in confidence. For children in trouble, need, or danger.
Freepost 1111
London N1 OBR
(24-hour helpline)
0800 1111

Childline for Children in Care: Telephone line for children

who are looked after in children's homes, foster homes, and
residential care. Calls are free, and do not appear on any
telephone bill.
Freepost 1111
London N1 OBR
Helpline 0800 884444

Childwatch: Tries to raise public and professional awareness
of the incidence of family violence and child abuse. It acts as a
referral agency for the counselling of adults who were abused
as children.
206 Hessle Road
Hull
North Humberside
HU3 3BE
0482 25552

Christian Survivors of Sexual Abuse (CSSA): National
office as well as local support group; letters only; offers
support and encouragement, advice and contact with other
survivors' groups, teaching, prayer and service. Organises a
national conference as well as local seminars for abused people
and those helping them; inter denominational.
BM CSSA
London
WCIN 3XX

Churches' Council for Health and Healing: Puts people
in touch with their local Christian healing ministry.
St Marylebone Parish Church
Marylebone Road
London NW 5LT
071 486 9644

Community Action Trust: Members of the public can ring
in anonymously and pass on to the police information about
any crime – including abuse.
Crimestoppers Freephone
08000 555111

Crusade for World Revival (CWR): Training courses for counsellors who are helping those who have been abused; counselling referral service – national network.
CWR
Waverley Abbey House
Waverley Lane
Farnham
Surrey GU9 8EP
0252 783695

Ellel Grange:
Christian healing and counselling centre; retreats for various needs, including sexual abuse; training courses for those helping people who have been abused.
Two centres:
1. Ellel Grange
Lancaster
LA2 OHN
0524 751 651
2. Glyndely Manor
Stone Cross
Pevensey
Nr Eastbourne
BN24 5BS
0323 440440

Emily Appeal Fund: Group of people with the common aim of raising funds to provide support and financial assistance for those who need therapeutic help because they have been abused.
0483 764666

Faithfull Foundation: Offers help to children who are being abused, adult survivors, non-offending parents, perpetrators of sexual abuse; assessment and ongoing individual therapy and group services.

Windmill House
Weatheroak Hill
Nr Aylechurch
Birmingham B48 7EA
0564 822448

Grace Ministries: Counselling and training counsellors; weekend training and workshops; supervision work for counsellors helping others.
Ron and Dorothy Dennis
PO Box 1500
Lancing
West Sussex BN15 0ZQ
0903 761477

Kidscape: Campaign for Child Safety: Tries to prevent abuse of children through education programmes; provides books, leaflets, video programmes, and free parent guides. Send large SAE.
152 Buckingham Palace Road
London SW1W 9TR
071 730 3300

London Healing Mission: Offers ministry and care for the whole person; counselling and prayer – face-to-face and telephone. Healing services, 9.45–1.00, 2.00–5.30 (except Thursdays when 11.15–3.00).
20 Dawson Place
London W2 4TJ
071 229 3641

London Women's Aid: 24-hour crisis line for women experiencing any kind of domestic violence; safe accommodation in refuges always available.
52–54 Featherstone Street
London EC1Y 8RT
071 251 6537
National Office
0272 633542

MOSAC (Mothers of Sexually Abused Children): Helpline run *by* mothers of abused children *for* mothers of abused children. Wednesday, 10.00–4.00, and answerphone service.
081 293 9990

NCH Action for Children (formerly **National Children's Homes**): Phone-in service for people with problems with children and families. Monday to Friday, 9.00–5.00.
071 226 2033

Parent Line: Telephone counselling service for carers under stress. They aim to prevent child abuse and the maltreatment of infants and young children; twenty-two groups nationwide. 24-hour answerphone service.
0268 757077

Parents Anonymous: A listening service for carers under stress who may be harming, or in danger of harming, their children. They can also refer to other related organisations.
071 272 2192

Portal Christian Rehabilitation Centre: Rehabilitative care for people between 18 and 35 who have suffered emotional, physical, or sexual abuse in childhood, and who have been in the long-term care of local authorities, psychiatric hospitals, or prisons. Open to anyone with or without religious persuasion.
5 Junction Road
Romford
Essex RM1 3QS
0708 741971

Rape Crisis Centres: Confidential support provided for women and girls who have experienced sexual violence either recently or in the past. They are autonomous groups, each offering a variety of services; centres nationwide.
London 071 837 1600
Belfast 0232 249696

Edinburgh 031 556 9437
Cardiff 0222 373181

Relate: Supports marriage and family life; counselling service;
contact to find local help; useful literature available.
Herbert Gray College
Little Church Street
Rugby CV21 3AP
0788 573241

Survivors: Offers advice and support mainly to male victims
of sexual abuse; telephone helpline, one-to-one counselling;
self-help groups mainly in London area; training for statutory
and non-statutory organisations. Tuesday, Wednesday and
Thursday evenings 7.00–10.00.
PO Box 2470
London W2 1NW
071 833 3737

WAMP (Women and Medical Practice): Health information; advice and counselling; tries to set up self-help groups.
Attempts to bridge the gap between the National Health
Service and the more general needs of the public.
40 Turnpike Lane
London N8 0PS
081 888 2782

Women and Girls Network: One-to-one counselling and
information service for women and girls who have experienced
any form of male violence. Also gives help to mothers; training
for other voluntary agencies; helps initiation of self-help groups
with varying emphases. Wednesday, 11.00–4.00.
London Women's Centre
Wesley House
4 Wild Court
London WC2B 5AU
071 978 8887